NO COUNTRY WOMAN

NO

ZOYA

COUNTRY

PATEL

WOMAN

hachette AUSTRALIA

Pseudonyms have been used in this book and other details altered where necessary to protect the identity and privacy of people mentioned. While every effort has been made to recall past events accurately, the memories contained within this book are the author's own and may differ from those of others.

hachette
AUSTRALIA

Published in Australia and New Zealand in 2018
by Hachette Australia
(an imprint of Hachette Australia Pty Limited)
Level 17, 207 Kent Street, Sydney NSW 2000
www.hachette.com.au

NATIONAL LIBRARY OF AUSTRALIA

A catalogue record for this book is available from the National Library of Australia

ISBN 978 0 7336 4006 3 (paperback)

Cover design by Astred Hicks
Author photo courtesy of Linda Macpherson
Typeset in 12.5/18.2 pt Adobe Garamond Pro by Bookhouse, Sydney
Printed and bound in Australia by McPherson's Printing Group

FSC www.fsc.org MIX Paper from responsible sources FSC® C001695

The paper this book is printed on is certified against the Forest Stewardship Council® Standards. McPherson's Printing Group holds FSC® chain of custody certification SA-COC-005379. FSC® promotes environmentally responsible, socially beneficial and economically viable management of the world's forests.

TO IKEBAL AND NAAZMEEN PATEL,
FOR ALL THAT THEY HAVE GIVEN ME

CONTENTS

NO-COUNTRY WOMAN

I was born in a hospital in Suva, Fiji. I can't recall ever seeing the building on my trips back to the city, first as a child and later as an adult. I imagine it in shades of blue and brown, the plastic waiting-room chairs covered in the fine film of moisture that creeps over everything there. It is not a place I've thought of often, but I think of it now and wonder how it has shaped me.

I am Fijian-Indian, and have lived in Australia since I was three years old, for 25 years of my life. Memories of my early life in Fiji are limited to flashes, like an old film projector running backwards. I remember a blue dress, a trip on a boat where my father handed me a dried, floating starfish that I clutched in my fingers, determined not to lose it back to the ocean.

There is a memory of a strange man coming to our house and giving me a stuffed toy koala. My mother has assured me the man was my father, returning to Fiji after a trip to Australia to scout it out as a possible home for us. I was clearly too young to remember him at the time, but 'Koala Patch' has been my companion ever since.

She was with me when we flew to Australia in 1992, to be greeted by colleagues from my father's new job at the local electricity company in Albury, in southwest New South Wales. She sat in my first bedroom, shared with all three of my siblings, in a rental house in Lavington, a suburb of Albury. She moved to Canberra with us in 1998, and suffered through multiple house moves, being packed and repacked, until I eventually packed her away for good with our other favourite childhood toys. It is funny to me that this symbol of Australia first came to me when I was still in Fiji, unaware that my birthplace would never truly be my home.

After several years of avoidance, I visited Fiji again in 2014, when I was 24 years old. It was the first time I'd gone back without my family, and the difference was emphasised by the fact that I was travelling with my partner, Chris, and his family and friends.

Leading up to the trip, I was plagued by anxiety. My relationship with my own family was complicated. Over the past several years, I had drifted further and further away from our culture and traditions, and the result was a stilted and distant connection to my parents and siblings at that time. This was the main reason I had been avoiding Fiji, because I had never travelled there without my family and doing so made it difficult to ignore the way our relationship had changed. Compounding this, Chris is white – making our relationship shocking and taboo for many Fijian-Indians, who believe in marrying within their own culture. I was certain that the staff at the luxury resort we'd booked, and other Indians we met, would judge me for stepping outside these strict boundaries. I knew it would feel strange to be the only non-white person in the Australian tourist party, being waited on by people who looked like me, and whose experiences I might have shared if my parents hadn't been able to migrate to Australia.

There was also a sense of guilt at how easily I had dismissed Fiji as a desirable place to visit up to that point. I had always resented visiting Fiji. Every year my parents would plan a trip back 'home'. We would spend weeks visiting family, battling the oppressive heat, going to functions and weddings, wearing Indian clothes and speaking only Hindi. I struggled with this forced cultural immersion, and it grew harder with each passing year. By the time I was a teenager, I spent all year trying to downplay my difference and fit in with my white Australian friends – dressing alternatively and highlighting my love of indie rock bands. Re-engaging with Fijian-Indian culture and dressing in traditional clothes seemed to require a denial of the 'Aussie' life I tried to live at home: summer afternoons at the pool, movies with my friends, all of us in jeans and t-shirts.

The thought of going to Fiji of my own accord seemed far-fetched. It was a journey I had always made with my family, something planned and organised by others. After my grandmother passed away in Fiji in 2011 I thought I would never go back. So when Chris's sister decided to hold her wedding in Fiji, I couldn't understand the appeal. I kept thinking of the heat and humidity, the tiny lizards that crawled up the walls of the rooms at night. Why wouldn't you have a nice wedding on the New South Wales south coast, where the weather was pleasant and the wi-fi fast?

But a part of me was also excited. On the days leading up to our departure, memories came flooding back: the smell of sugar cane fields after harvest; the sticky vinyl seats on public buses with no glass in the windows, DIY air-conditioned; the mushy texture of *dalo* (taro) after being cooked for hours in the *lovo* fire pit. Despite my resistance, my childhood experiences of Fiji had seeped under my skin, and these memories came with a burst of nostalgia. I also remembered how it felt to walk down a street in Suva and blend in with the crowd. It was a sense of anonymity I craved but never experienced in Australia, and I had only recently begun to realise how much of my energy every day went into appearing ordinary when my skin colour stood out like a beacon, especially in the white suburbia of affluent Canberra.

I was nervous to be returning to Fiji, but there was a pull, a strange sense of homecoming I hadn't experienced before. When the trip finally arrived, I was on edge. 'I know it might be weird to be back,' Chris said on the plane, and I nodded, but he couldn't possibly understand what it really felt like. As we landed I felt a rush of conflicting emotions – anxiety and excitement, and a nostalgia that I felt deep in my bones when I looked out the plane window to see the green hills rising to meet us. An air-conditioned bus took us from the airport in Nadi to Port Denarau, where a water taxi waited. The streets slipped by, the lush green leafery that sprawls across every visible piece of land in Fiji creeping to the sides of the road, trailing up the corners of buildings. On the bus was our twenty-person wedding party, all in high spirits at the beginning of our week away. Everyone was Caucasian – except me. My skin is brown, my hair the same frizzy black as that of the Fijians (both Indian and *kaiviti* – indigenous Fijian) who walked along the footpaths past sleepy stores, who stood at bus stops with distracted expressions, or who played energetic games of rugby on the ovals we drove past.

It felt strange to be sitting on the bus while everyone who looked like me was on the other side of the window, occupying a world completely unlike mine. I tried to feel a sense of connection. Everything looked familiar but nothing struck a chord. Fiji was my home for three years of my life. It was where I took my first steps, learned my first words. Where two grandfathers and a grandmother lived and died, where my parents were born and where they lived for more than half of their lives. Watching the distant hills slip out of view as we drove, I had an overwhelming sense of displacement. How could a place be so central to everything that had made me and still feel so unknown? The bus paused at an intersection and I watched a young *kaiviti* man walk down the street. He looked up and our eyes caught for a moment. He smiled and waved, and I waved back.

The wedding party was staying on Vomo, a privately owned island in the Mamanuca region, all verdant foliage, white sand and sprawling coral reefs in the shadow of Mount Vomo, which rises on the eastern side of the island. This was a part of Fiji I had never seen before.

I was apprehensive as our water taxi pulled onto the beach. A waiting party of *kaiviti* staff sang to us as we were helped off the boat. It made me feel uneasy to see their grass skirts, the hibiscus flowers behind every ear, the practised way they all shouted '*Bula!*' in greeting. The commercialisation of *kaiviti* culture felt uncomfortable and inauthentic to me, and I worried that by participating in the morally fraught tourism industry in Fiji, I was contributing to the broader issue of indigenous cultures being tokenised the world over.

Fiji was colonised in 1874 by the British, and after protests in England against the use of indigenous Fijians as labourers off the back of the anti-slavery movement, *kaiviti* culture was 'preserved' in a way that ultimately eroded the ability of the native people to have any control over the use of their lands for economic gain. The use of indentured labourers from India further complicated this, particularly when, at times, the Indian migrant population has represented almost half of the total population of Fiji. When the country eventually attained independence from British rule in 1970, Fiji was left in a state of disruption – Fijian-Indians were stranded far from their homeland, and native Fijians were still struggling to reclaim theirs. The country has a long history of political and racial unrest, which continues in different ways today. To be an Indian in Fiji is complicated, and being a Fijian-Indian-Australian is even more complicated.

Having the Fijian staff serve me, a fellow brown person – carrying my bags and offering me a wet towel and a drink – was more awkward than I expected. I had somehow crossed the white–brown barrier to the side of privilege, a position that I battle against in Australia every time I take a cab driven by an Indian man or see an Indian woman cleaning the floors at my local shopping centre. *Why me and not them?* I often think. If we had stayed in Fiji I would probably be working at a resort or in my parents' small business. Perhaps, if I was lucky, I would have been able to study teaching or business administration at TAFE. Luck and circumstance mean that I have a university education, an Australian passport and a middle-class lifestyle.

My guilt is amplified every time I visit my cousins in Fiji, whose parents tried for years to migrate to New Zealand or Australia but were unlucky with the timing. Migration laws in Australia are an ever-tightening noose, making it harder and harder for migrants unable to satisfy Australian skill shortages to obtain visas. Whenever I stayed at my uncle's house in Suva, where two of my cousins shared a tiny bedroom with my grandmother, and my uncle earned as little as two dollars an hour driving a taxi, my guilt would plague me, manifesting in the books and clothes and Australian lollies we brought as gifts.

At Vomo this guilt became a constant, uncomfortable buzz in my ears. I overcompensated by rushing to carry my own bags, saying 'thank you' too much and smiling in an over-the-top, almost pained way. I couldn't accept my role as pampered tourist, not in the country that had produced me only a few degrees of opportunity from the *kaiviti* staff at the resort.

On the first night there was a traditional *kava* welcoming ceremony. The staff brewed the pungent, mildly sedative drink while the guests looked on. They stirred the *kava*, explaining its cultural significance, and came around to offer everyone a taste. The other guests were excited to be there, enthusiastic to learn about *kava*. I sat towards the back of the group. For me, *kava* wasn't some novelty at an island resort. It was a drug that I had seen consume the lives of men that my family knew in Fiji, becoming a constant escape from their daily lives. Growing up, I knew not to look when certain male family members got up after dinner and disappeared to the porch with their *kava*, bowl and cheesecloth. It wasn't forbidden to talk about, but I knew my mother and father disapproved, and *kava* took on a sinister quality. With *kava* available throughout Fiji and consumed without much thought for the long-term health consequences (like liver damage), addiction was rife but largely ignored.

Chris's sister sipped from the cup and passed it to me. 'Are you going to try it? It makes my tongue feel a little numb!'

I smiled back. 'I think I'll pass.'

Chris reached an arm around me, squeezing my shoulder briefly, and I knew he could tell I was tense. But how could I explain to him the layers of complexity that this simple, touristy ceremony held for Fijians and Fijian-Indians? The disconnect between these elements of Fijian culture that were on display for tourists and the realities of life for average Fijians was so stark in that moment. I couldn't enjoy the grass skirts, the warrior dances, the *kava* ceremony in the same way because they were markers of my birthplace, of a culture to which I once belonged, one burdened with an unstable political system, a problematic history built on slavery and racial tensions, and a widening gap between the rich and the poor.

As a Fijian-Indian, I was also the unwilling beneficiary of the subjugation of *kaiviti* people, and now a migrant twice over who had benefited from each move. What right did I have to enjoy the entertainment value of this ceremony, when it spoke to a more insidious issue of the disempowerment of the *kaiviti* people? How could I join in with Chris' family and friends without colluding in the tourism industry that reaped the profits from this oppression, profits which very rarely trickled down to the *kaiviti* locals? I spent the evening in a tense almost-silence, determined not to ruin the event for the group but increasingly worried about the rest of the trip.

Our villa at Vomo was the highest on the island, set against the back of the mountain. I was surprised by the lack of frogs and lizards on the island. 'On the mainland, you can barely walk anywhere without stepping on a frog,' I told Chris. But was that true? Maybe frogs and lizards were a seasonal plague – I had almost always come to Fiji during summer. Or maybe it was something to do with the ecosystem on Vomo in particular. I didn't know the answer. My uncertainty made me uneasy, a reminder that I might be *from* Fiji but I wasn't really *of* Fiji.

So many of the 'memories' I had of Fiji were actually stories told to me by my parents and grandparents, which my mind had then embellished into scenes as if from a movie. I could almost see my father skipping school to take his dog to the river for a swim, or hear my mother squealing after she accidentally pushed her brother out of a second-storey window during a sibling spat. (He was fine, but the story became legend.) My impressions of Fiji are a merging of my own visits and my family's collective remembrances, to the point where I can't tell what is true memory and what is imagined. What did I really know about Fiji, in the end?

The view from our balcony at Vomo was distinctly Fijian, and breathtaking – the sea a smooth expanse, with the distant shadowy form of another island on the horizon, and palm trees and foliage covering the near ground. I stood out there in the morning, drinking it in. I yearned to connect to this country again.

Spending each day with the wedding party, listening as they raved about what they saw, made me feel a strange wash of pride, unfamiliar to me when it came to Fiji. 'This country is so beautiful,' they would say. 'It's heavenly.' Each compliment they paid to Fiji felt like it was somehow directed at me and the thousands of others born in the country, even though I knew that in reality it had little to do with me. I couldn't take pride in a country that I barely knew, but I wanted to – I wanted to feel the same confidence in my connection to Fiji that I could see in the staff, and in my parents when we visited together. I wanted to feel at ease in this country that had made me, but it still felt alien, foreign.

Barely any of the staff on the island had asked me where I was from – they were almost all *kaiviti* and they simply accepted me as part of the Australian wedding party. Perhaps they assumed I was married to Chris, and took it for granted that my life was miles away from theirs, both literally and figuratively. One waiter asked me where I was from as he served me at dinner, and was excited to hear I'd been born in Suva. There was none of the judgement I'd been expecting as a Fijian-Indian girl with a white partner.

In Australia, Chris and I have become used to sideways looks and even open hostility from Indian-Australians who see our relationship as an aberration, the worst kind of breaking of cultural codes. It is considered scandalous in South Asian cultures for women to be with white men, or men who aren't obviously from the same background. Although most white Australians barely spare us a second glance, we have experienced rudeness from Indian waiters, checkout staff and taxi drivers, usually accompanied by a snide comment about my race. I was expecting similar reactions at Vomo, but no one seemed to notice or care. I was just another paying guest.

I was surprised and entranced by this version of Fiji. The carefully constructed environment of the resort – three gourmet meals every day, the sun playing along the coastline, the polite, measured tone of our interactions with staff – was enchanting. Fiji felt inviting, alluring even. The complete separation of Vomo from the realities of life elsewhere in Fiji had worked its magic. Away from the streets, the poverty and poor infrastructure, the judgemental gaze of Fijian-Indians, I found a sort of peace with my birthplace that I hadn't had before. I knew it was a peace built on false foundations, but I felt almost belligerent in my acceptance of the fake Fijian culture that Vomo reflected at me. Why couldn't I just take this one island as a representation of all of Fiji, like the white Australians in our party could? Why couldn't I have the island paradise without the cultural complexities and economic difficulties?

For once, I wanted my connection to Fiji to be simple, based on the here and now, and not on the generations of history that I carried in my DNA. Determined to find a positive, I wilfully ignored the fragility of the link I had made. Chris and I talked about coming back, just the two of us. We could make our trip what we want it to be, I said. I could have a connection to my birthplace without having to engage with every aspect of the culture.

By the final day of our stay at the resort, I felt a swelling of affection for Fiji. For so many years I had battled the part of my identity that originated here. At first because I wanted to fit in with my white Australian friends, and later because of my family's unhappiness with my choices, I assumed that I would never be welcome in Fijian-Indian culture again. But Vomo had changed all of that. This Fiji was an accepting one, without the cultural conditions I had come to expect. It might have been a connection with a false construct, with a product of the country's powerful and primarily foreign-owned tourism industry, but it felt meaningful at the time. As we left Vomo, I decided I didn't have to give up this connection. I told myself I could be both Australian and Fijian-Indian, without losing something in between the two cultures.

On the last day of the trip, we travelled back to Nadi to stay the night before an early-morning flight to Sydney. It was late afternoon when we arrived and were driven to our hotel. The city looked more like the Fiji I remembered – the crumbling, crooked streets, the dusty air. The further we got from the airport, the more real it looked in contrast to the shiny veneer of the resort.

I was still filled with my newfound love for the country and we decided to go exploring in Nadi town. I said I wanted to see the 'true' Fiji before we left. My sense of Fiji was formed from my memories of Suva, Rakiraki and Lautoka, where my family was from and where I had spent those childhood trips. I expected Nadi to feel familiar somehow, even though I had spent little time there.

Chris, his brother and I set out for town in a taxi. The driver was Indian, and he barely glanced at me as we clambered into the back. He chatted with the boys, asking them where they were from. When one mentioned that I was born in Fiji, the driver's tone changed. 'Yeah? In Suva? Which suburb did you live in?' He sounded almost aggressive, as if testing me.

I opened and closed my mouth. I had no idea what the suburbs in Suva were called. I had been there so many times but the geography of the city was unknown to me. We just went wherever my parents took us. I could pick out my uncle's house from a line-up, but I couldn't direct a taxi driver there for the life of me. I tried to ignore the hostility in the driver's voice, the challenge behind the question: *Prove it – prove you're more like me than you are like them.* It was probably the harmless rivalry of a local seeking to place me within the hierarchy of Suva's neighbourhoods, but it reminded me of the tenuous link I had with the country. Some of the peace I'd found at Vomo began to wear off.

When we got to the town centre we started walking the streets, glancing into shop windows. It was a slightly desperate attempt to find something 'authentic' in what is basically a shopping district in an airport city. The atmosphere on the street was not friendly – gone was the measured politeness of the *kaiviti* staff on Vomo. Indian shop owners stared at me, then took in my two white, male companions, judgement clear in their eyes. Some called out as we passed, ignoring me and inviting the boys to view trinkets and Hawaiian shirts.

Then a young man yelled out, staring at me, 'Where are you from?'

Without thinking, I said, 'I was born here.'

He sneered, and glanced at the boys. 'You don't look like you're from Fiji.'

We walked away. Did he mean that I didn't look like I was from Fiji, or that Chris and his brother didn't? Did I not look like I was from Fiji *because* I was with Chris? I felt jarred, out of place. I longed to see something familiar – my grandparents' farmhouse with its broad front verandah. The small bridge we had to cross in Suva to reach the cinema. My uncle's old house with the steep concrete path we would trail up single file after a day of shopping. But we were hours from Suva or Rakiraki, and I felt light-years away from those memories. Despite my desire to discover Fiji for myself, the uncertainty I felt that afternoon in Nadi forced me to acknowledge that my only real connection to Fiji was through my family.

What did I really know about life in Fiji that wasn't gleaned from my parents? When we visited, my mother and father visibly relaxed, as if they could finally let out a breath they had held in for too long. They slipped back into their Fijian identities with ease: Dad would rattle off words in *kaiviti* and Mum's gestures loosened, taking on the animated physicality I could see in my aunts and other women who were used to operating in the brisk, energetic pace of Suva. For my parents, the veneer is 'acting' Australian, whereas for me, I was swiftly realising, anything other than Australia was foreign. Fiji only felt like home in the artificial environment of Vomo, or within the safe confines of family homes. On my own, I was lost.

We caught another taxi back to the hotel. My head was roiling with conflicted thoughts. Those few hours in Nadi had brought me thudding back to earth. The connection I had felt on the island was false, created by the customer service of a tourist resort. No amount of politeness could recover what I had lost by disconnecting from Fijian-Indian culture. I was now the Other, the example parents use to warn their daughters.

I remembered hearing a relative say once at a family gathering, about a girl who had married a white man: 'She'll be an outcast in our culture.' For most Indian migrants, 'our culture' was mutually exclusive of whatever western culture we resided within. It referred only to the traditions we – migrants from numerous countries within the broader Indian diaspora – had brought from our home countries, and which we had to constantly push against mainstream society to maintain in our adopted home. But for me, 'our culture' felt forced, a society and a set of rules that didn't apply to me. I'd always felt that my parents' insistence that we visit Fiji every year was a sort of immunisation against becoming too westernised. In my case, it had clearly failed.

When my relationship with my parents had grown constrained, though, and the realities of being an 'outcast' became apparent in the judgement of strangers, I realised the loss I had dealt myself by stepping so far away from my cultural heritage. I would never again sit anonymously at the back of a wedding hall, soaking in the music and laughter. Nothing about me could be anonymous now, as news of my partner spread through our small community in Australia. I was caught firmly between the different countries I was made from.

In Nadi that afternoon, I had my first experience of ostracism in a setting where I had previously always blended in. I felt more conspicuous and uncomfortable as I walked with Chris than I had ever felt in Australia as the only non-white person in a room.

The taxi driver we had on the way back to the hotel was openly rude, refusing to look at me and complaining about his job, his terrible wages, the need to survive off tips from passengers. His tone was bitter and his dislike of all three of us – foreigners that we were – was palpable. I sat in the back seat, my teeth gritted. I remember thinking, *This man is odious, but he isn't lying when he says he earns two dollars an hour and can't afford to visit his daughter in Australia.* Despite his rudeness to me, I knew I would give him a tip.

When we arrived at the hotel he told us the fare was ten dollars, so I gave him twenty. He looked at me for the first time. 'For me?'

I nodded and climbed out of the car. He looked a little startled, perhaps a bit embarrassed. 'Thank you,' he said.

That night I lay in our sterile hotel room and cried as I tried to explain why the afternoon had upset me so deeply. Chris was concerned, but also confused – why did I want so much to belong here? Why did it matter, when my home is Australia, when *I* am Australian?

'You don't know how much it means to go somewhere where everyone looks like you,' I said. 'To not be the only brown person in the room, or one of three brown people on the bus.'

I wanted to fit in, to belong in Fiji. Maybe I just wanted to prove that I hadn't lost my heritage through the life I had chosen as an adult. The Nigerian author Ijeoma Umebinyuo writes in her poem 'Diaspora Blues' of the dual foreignness that is the identity of second-generation migrants – caught between two countries, neither of which can fully accept us. When I first read that poem, it was like a punch to the heart – here, at last, was articulated the strange sense of 'unbelonging' that I have felt my whole life but have never been able to fully understand.

Being Fijian-Indian is a constant marker of my difference in Australia. But being Australian precludes me from ever truly belonging in Fiji or India. My lived experiences are influenced by all these facets of my cultural identity, to the extent that it is forged more out of difference than from any connection to the three countries that have created me. I am not of any one country but am a true mix, unable to separate the strands of each culture. As Umebinyuo writes, my foreignness is as obvious as it is intangible, in each of the three settings.

I am a no one, a no-country woman.

The fact is, other than looking different, my experiences of being Fijian-Indian in Australia have been primarily marked not by cultural differences worthy of celebration but by what I *couldn't* do. Yes, I ate different food growing up, and went to Indian weddings, and spoke Hindi at home. But for me, those things didn't encapsulate 'being Fijian-Indian' as much as all the 'Australian' things I wasn't allowed to do: going to sleepovers at friends' houses, dating, wearing certain clothes, listening to certain music. When I thought of myself as Fijian-Indian, it was more as a marker of my being 'not Australian', or not *really* Australian.

Of course, as an adult I can see the value of the cultural immersion my parents created for us, despite being so far from home. I can also see how their rules for us were based on a desire to protect us, and were built on their values, which hold family as central to life. I now feel a wistfulness for Fijian-Indian culture, and the way it imbued my childhood and adolescence. I am grateful for the lessons my parents gave us to help us understand our heritage, and, in a way, to understand them and how they came to be the people they are. But those positive experiences paled in comparison to the day-to-day alienation I often felt growing up in Australia. And when we were in Fiji or India, this sense of alienation was simply recalibrated for the environment – never have I experienced the sort of easy cultural belonging I imagine is felt by those who live in the countries that match their cultural heritage.

When I think about it, I don't even know what 'belonging' in Fiji would mean for me, considering that the norms of Fijian-Indian culture are so often at loggerheads with my personal beliefs and value system. My personal code of ethics and my feminism have largely grown out of my frustration at the gender norms within Fijian-Indian culture as I experienced it. It's hard for me to unpick what part of these norms was Indian, or Fijian, or Muslim, or whether it was just a particular world view that emerged from a mix of all of those influences, but I always found it difficult to marry the independence I yearned for, and the strength and confidence my parents encouraged in us, with the more conservative expectations of the broader culture in Fiji, which reinforce the role of women within the domestic sphere, and of men as patriarchs of a family.

But 'belonging' in Australia isn't as simple as taking on 'Australian values' (whatever that means) either. I spend my days in Australia fielding questions from mostly (though not always) well-meaning strangers about where I'm 'from', where I'm 'really from' and what my 'background' is. I look different, therefore I am different – it's the assumption most people act on.

Different from what, though? In my hometown of Canberra, thousands of people are shades of brown and olive, showing the diversity of the population. And Indigenous Australians, the first to occupy this land, can never be the norm in a country that at best ignores them, and at worst systematically tried to eradicate them. So who am I different from? Although the whitewashed media portrays a different image, Australia is many shades of colours – a fact I sometimes forget when faced with the small acts of racism that filter through my daily life. These incidents are discombobulating, but also infrequent; if anything, the unbelonging I feel in Australia is driven by my desire to somehow bridge this gap between my heritage and my true identity despite the connection feeling false, instead of just letting go and allowing myself to be the mixture of cultural influences that I am.

In travelling back to Fiji, I thought that if I could just find a point of connection with the country where I was born, perhaps my unending questions about my cultural core could be laid to rest – and my life in Australia would become easier too. But fabricating a sense of connection with Fiji from six days spent on an island resort was impossible – not surprisingly, given that 24 years of visiting the country hadn't. The Fiji I experienced on Vomo was as fake as the Fiji thousands of Australian tourists experience every year that convinces them the 'island paradise' they see is a true depiction of the country.

In reality, of course, no culture is static; every culture is always in flux, and similarly identity is ever moving, ever changing. Perhaps there will be times in my life when my Indian self or my Fijian self will come more to the fore. In fact, I enjoy picturing a renewed closeness to India and to Fiji as I get older. I like the idea of travelling to both countries with my parents as they age, and finally finding time to ask all the questions I have always wondered about, and to hear the stories they are yet to tell me. I don't think this will necessarily draw me closer to my cultural roots, but rather that as I grow and change I will be more able to open up to the cultures that have influenced me without judgement or a fear of losing something from one by connecting with the other.

My identity is more complex than where I live, where I was born, where my ancestors came from. It is made up of the people I belong to, the houses where I have had my big thoughts, and the places across the world that have made my breath catch.

THE LABOUR OF A MIGRANT

If you're a member of a minority group, it can be hard to admit when a cultural stereotype has a grain of truth to it. Every stereotype is based on some element of fact, though the often discriminatory tone of racial caricatures is usually born of deep-seated prejudice.

One of the most pervasive stereotypes of Indian immigrants the world over is that of the Indian small-business owner, the savvy, stingy subcontinental with a cockroach-like ability to thrive in any environment, who infiltrates a milkbar or service station and takes over entirely, unable to be dislodged as they feed off the economy they have adopted.

There is nothing noble about this stereotype. This is no success story or aspirational narrative. There is no suggestion of a family working hard, providing for themselves and making a life in a new country. We are not entrepreneurs like white small-business owners. We are as irritating as the Indian mynah bird, a highly efficient invasive species that decimates native populations in its non-natural habitat.

I have always felt a twinge of embarrassment when confronted with this stereotype in popular culture, or in casual jokes made by acquaintances. If there's one family that matches the image of the prolific Indian business owner, it's mine.

So far, my parents have owned and run six businesses. The first was a charcoal chicken shop on the main street in Albury. My parents bought the shop after they had spent a few years in Australia working in their day jobs, Dad as an engineer, and Mum in a supermarket. Mum ran the business while Dad continued working full-time, helping her in the evenings, and we all made it work. Within a few months, the business had added a new menu of Indian curries alongside the existing charcoal chicken fare, to the delight of our regulars. Every day at lunchtime, Mum dropped off hot, delicious chicken sandwiches or curry and roti parcels to us at school, and after school we did our homework in the small office/rec room at the back of the shop.

When I was ten we moved to Canberra, where my parents ran a business selling imported furniture for a while, before buying their first motel a year later. There wasn't an obvious pattern to their business choices – it was about what attracted them with its sense of opportunity, and what would be flexible to manage around their young family.

That first motel was a small, ten-room business with a house attached. The house had only two bedrooms and one bathroom, but my parents put up a curtain to turn half of the lounge room into their bedroom. I shared a room with my sixteen-year-old brother, Zaved, a complete saint for putting up with his little sister, who had so many stuffed toys that a hammock had to be constructed over her bed to hold them all. My sisters, Zaheeda (thirteen) and Zakia (eleven), shared the other bedroom. As a family, we try never to talk about that time of adolescent conflict, yelling and blasting 1990s pop music. When the line for the bathroom was too long, we would use the nearest vacant motel bathroom, being sure to take a cleaning kit with us and put it to rights after.

'A family business means everyone helps out,' Mum used to say, and we did. Weekends meant everyone pitching in to help clean the rooms, so our full-time cleaners had their days off. Some of my best memories of that time are of splitting into cleaning teams and listening to music, joking and laughing as we worked. Zaheeda and Zaved helped on reception, and Zakia and I spent a lot of lazy summer afternoons in the pool. It was pretty wonderful.

After a few years, we moved into a house nearby and sold the motel, before buying another, bigger one – 30 rooms on one of the major streets in Queanbeyan, just outside Canberra. This time we renovated the attached home, above the motel dining hall. It was still very cramped – Zaved, somehow always the one to draw the short straw, made a bedroom out of what had been the tiny kitchen space, but he never complained. We all still helped out with cleaning on the weekends, and Zakia and I were promoted to reception as well. Hilariously, I insisted on only being paid the award wage (instead of the more generous wage my parents offered) and receiving a weekly pay slip. I wanted my job to be as legitimate as those my friends had started at the local Subway or McDonald's, not just a favour from my parents.

'You seriously want me to do a timesheet and a pay slip for you every week?' my long-suffering mother asked at the commencement of my new 'job'.

I nodded. 'Just treat me like a regular employee.' Looking back, I'm pretty sure normal employees didn't get to read Harry Potter fanfiction while on reception.

After about two years living onsite, we moved into a separate house. My daily interaction with the motel ended at that point, and I moved on to other part-time jobs, but my parents still own the business, although it's now operated by a full-time manager.

In addition to the motel, my parents own a cafe and a commercial farm. They had intended to buy a small rural plot to live on and enjoy their retirement, with room for a handful of chooks and somewhere for the grandkids to play, but this somehow turned into a 75-acre farm that produces a commercial quantity of vegetables each year. My dad is in his element as a farmer, a far cry from his decades working in an office. I like to see him out and about on the weekends, tending his vegetables and running his team of staff. It's not exactly 'retirement', though.

I joke with my friends that my parents are incapable of relaxing. There was a very brief period when Mum wasn't working except for keeping oversight of the motel, and Dad was 'only' working full-time as an engineer, and they both seemed deflated. 'It's so boring,' Mum said about her days of reading and chilling out. Most people dream of free time, but my parents need to be doing something challenging to feel happy. Now, with the farm and the cafe, they're in their element.

Both my parents are whip-smart, hardworking and always looking for the next challenge. But their drive and business acumen are not just a quirk of their personalities. The desire of many Fijian-Indians to run a business and the work ethic needed to do so effectively are tied to the history of colonialism in Fiji. Since the country attained independence, its economy has been slow to grow and subject to the uncertainties of an unstable democracy. Opportunities for social mobility are limited, and small business is one of the most accessible ways for people to earn more than the average wage and carve out better possibilities for their children. The uncertainty of being raised in a country with a much leaner economy and a far less stable political system instilled in my parents the need for self-sufficiency. In a system that could only offer a small number of white-collar jobs (often with an undertone of nepotism), the attraction of small business is clear.

For most of our family in Fiji, the objective of their work was always to find a way to migrate to a first-world country where wages were higher and there were more chances to get ahead. In Australia, the opportunities are multiplied. With four young children, my parents didn't want to be just comfortable, able to fund their basic needs (as they could have been if they had lived on their salaries alone); they wanted to build the economic stability that would allow them to experience the most of life, and give their children the best chance to succeed.

It's taken me more than 25 years to realise that my own manic work ethic – which sees me taking on numerous projects at once, with never a moment free – is a direct inheritance of their entrepreneurial spirit. I can now feel pride in their hard work and what they've achieved, but for most of my life I felt embarrassed about how different our family was from my friends' families, and the way we all worked so hard on our businesses instead of having an 'ordinary', laid-back Australian lifestyle.

My parents could literally never escape their work, because we lived adjacent to it. Dinner was regularly interrupted by the motel reception bell ringing. Holidays had to be planned around organising temporary relief to run the business. The workload was immense, and the pressure constant.

In popular culture, when a white family owns a business, it's usually something glitzy and glamorous. In the 1998 film *The Parent Trap*, for example, the twins' estranged parents are both supposedly business owners – the mother a fashion designer and the father a wine producer. Yet you don't see them staying up late doing the books, or running around with a rake or a pair of fabric scissors in hand. They are always swanning through an immaculate reception hall answering questions from anxious-to-please staff, or strolling the manicured grape arbours in a spotless shirt and jeans. Somehow they manage to own beautiful properties and have no financial worries, and still have time for their children.

When migrants with businesses are represented in pop culture, they are not glamorous. Instead, they are to some extent belittled by their own efforts, unable to fully enjoy the benefits of their businesses. It's gritty and grimy, and uncomfortable to watch, as if there is something greedy or uncouth in their business zeal. This disdain for migrants' obsession with customers and profits is representative of a broader cultural attitude towards migrant business owners.

When I started high school, I became increasingly embarrassed by my family's businesses. When my parents asked us kids to pitch in and help repaint motel rooms, I rolled my eyes, seeing it as an affront to my independence, as well as somewhat humiliating – I believed that white motel owners would just hire someone. If I had to clean the rooms on the weekend, I convinced myself that the white guests probably thought we were illegal immigrants, and that we should have tried to look more professional rather than wearing old tracksuit pants and t-shirts.

Arbitrarily, I had decided that the way we ran the motel was out of touch with modern practices. Snooty guests made me anxious, and I thought we must have confirmed their beliefs about the inferiority of the Indian race. I was afraid of racism, and I projected this fear onto my family and, by extension, everything my family did. Why couldn't both my parents just work in the public service like so many of my friends' parents? I would wonder. Maybe that would make us seem more normal, more *white*.

I now realise that my assumption that all white-owned businesses were intrinsically 'better' than my family's enterprises was illogical. Even when I went to rundown cafes or motels owned by white people and noticed things (dirty bathrooms, stodgy food) that would have embarrassed me had they occurred in my parents' businesses (not that they would have), my internalised shame as a migrant meant that I didn't question their superiority to our business practices.

What I chose not to think about as a teenager was how significantly our lives had been altered by my parents' hard work. We had gone from buying our furniture and most other household goods second-hand, and shopping regularly at bargain stores, to being able to redecorate our house, go on lovely holidays and generally have more freedom to enjoy life. We took more overseas holidays, and somewhere along the line I started to take it for granted that if ever I needed it, my parents would always have the means to bail me out. Rather than feeling pride in and gratitude for their efforts,

I developed the entitlement shown by many children with wealthy parents. I am appalled at myself now.

And yet my negative attitude towards our business success was not created in a vacuum. In fact, it was reflected at me again and again, through small, niggling gestures and attitudes displayed by white people we interacted with. On more than one occasion, a white guest would walk into reception and ask my mother, who was usually tidying the area or filing paperwork, if they could speak with the manager or owner. When she told them they were speaking to her, they would never apologise, and often expressed disbelief. Once, a guest walked straight past my mother and started speaking to our white cleaners, assuming they were in charge.

When interactions with guests or customers turned ugly, it almost always took a racist tone. My parents tended to shrug this off, confident that the arseholes were outnumbered by the nice guests, but it seeded in me a sense of racial hierarchy, and perversely made me want to win the approval of the faceless white masses even more. 'Who cares what they think of us,' my father would say. 'At the end of the day, what matters is who we are as people.' It was a good mantra, but I lacked their confidence and the negative experiences grated on me.

While I was at university, I worked in a pharmacy owned and run by an Indian man. His name was Rajesh but he called himself Bob, because he didn't want to have to deal with people not knowing how to say his name. Practically every day I worked there, someone would ask me if Rajesh was my father. Because, you know, two Indians in close proximity, even in a professional environment, are probably related. That we looked nothing alike (in fact, we were from different regions and cultures entirely) made no difference.

I saw the way Rajesh interacted with his customers, and felt a pang on his behalf. The jokey, overfriendly way he treated some white men revealed a sense of self-preservation, an instinctive knowledge that some people were more likely to create trouble. It is a sixth sense people of colour acquire to identify who feels threatened by your success in relation to your skin colour, versus those who don't even consider the two to be related.

When I took these subtle examples of racial prejudice and applied them to my own perspective, I started loading the idiosyncrasies of my parents as business owners as being examples of everything the white gaze implied – their inferiority, their strangeness, their unprofessionalism. When my father insisted on doing all of our repairs and plumbing himself, I didn't see this as thriftiness and an example of how capable he is, but as Indian stinginess. When our visiting relatives stayed in the motel rooms instead of in our house, and wandered around the complex, comfortable in their traditional clothes, I didn't recognise this as a rational use of space by my parents, but as a fresh-off-the-boat display of a lack of boundaries. When white guests displayed unconscious prejudice in their interactions with my family, I didn't feel anger at their racism; instead I felt a silent flush of shame at the differences my family exhibited.

What I didn't realise, or even have the perspective to begin to examine, was the fact that our cultural differences have indeed influenced our approach to small business – but only in positive ways.

To be a small-business owner takes a lot of resolve and self-motivation, two things my parents have in spades. Business is not for the faint-hearted. There is nothing glamorous about working 24 hours a day, seven days a week, always pinching pennies in the knowledge that success today can be gone tomorrow, and having to live and breathe the day-to-day running of your venture in order to make it work.

And the rewards can be small, at least in the early years. Just because this week's profit is high doesn't mean that next week's will be. Making a steady income from your business doesn't stop the flow of anxiety that courses through your veins. Add to that the pressures of raising four children, living in a different country from your place of birth, and (in the case of my father) working a separate full-time job on top of your small business, and you can begin to see the sheer magnitude of my parents' achievements.

When I asked my parents what drew them to small business, Dad shrugged. 'You have to be in it to win it. Why work for someone else when you can work for yourself?' There was no plan B – they threw everything they had into each venture, and as a result, each one was successful. It required a great deal of dedication and the ability to maintain an untenable workload and to work constantly towards a greater purpose.

When we owned our first motel, my mother was diagnosed with rheumatoid arthritis. A debilitating, degenerative autoimmune condition, it severely affects her mobility: she can only walk a few hundred metres at a time without experiencing pain, and needs to sit and rest frequently. And yet she never stopped doing the motel's laundry, running the financial side of the business, cooking and delivering breakfasts, and also being an incredibly present parent – she picked us up from school, took us to our extracurricular activities, organised holidays and fun activities on the weekend, and generally kept the family running.

When I consider the challenges that my parents faced and overcame, I am amazed – but not surprised. The primary variable in a small business is the owner's competence and ability; businesses can thrive or fail based on this factor alone. My parents only had each other to rely on, which made them fiercely independent of other people's help, and committed to each venture they chose. Most importantly, there is not a single ounce of entitlement in their make-up. Mum has often said to me, 'I don't care what job you do, as long as you're a good person. But everything we have in this life is earned, not given to us.'

We have to work hard for our dreams, otherwise life will likely pass us by without our realising it. It is a mantra I have taken on with fervour. Following this principle, I worked three jobs and three volunteer positions while studying full-time at university towards my undergraduate degree. It has also given me the drive to push hard in my communications career and in my writing. I have always set goals for myself in both of these areas, with a clear sense of what I want to achieve each year.

For a long time I didn't think my approach to work was unusual, until I grew old enough to see how differently I, and a segment of my peers, approached art and work, as compared to the mainstream. It is unsurprising to me that the majority of this group are from migrant backgrounds or grew up in a single-parent household, which I imagine produces similar resilience. We are self-driven and often hard on ourselves, and rarely procrastinate. I know that I can't enjoy my relaxation time if I haven't completed all the tasks on my to-do list (which is extensive and colour-coded). Written down, my habits make me sound like a run-of-the-mill Type A personality, but I think it's more than this. I am desperate to succeed in my plans and ventures, because my success is linked closely to my parents' legacy – what I achieve is a reflection of what they have achieved, and the doors they have opened for us.

The proof of their work will be in the outcomes for their children. Already, my siblings have carved this path ahead of me. All three are accomplished, driven, talented and successful in their fields. Importantly, for all of us, our motivation is largely self-generated, created from our interests and passion. This is another result of my parents' approach to work. They always encouraged us to pursue a career path that we enjoy, because working in jobs we hate is a waste of a life. In fact, while in some ways my parents do comply with stereotypes of Indian families, they certainly don't fit the stereotype of Indian parents who are obsessed with their children's academic achievements and want them to be doctors. They are the opposite – expecting us to motivate ourselves throughout school, and emphasising that the only person negatively affected by our failures would be ourselves.

As well as our reputation as stingy and cunning business owners, another insidious interpretation of the work ethic of the Indian diaspora is our new status as one of the 'model migrant' groups. Where once our business smarts were mocked, now they are applauded as a way to cast shade on other, 'less desirable' migrant groups. Despite seeming like a positive change in attitudes, this brief respite from racist caricatures has the negative effect of erasing the centuries of marginalisation faced by immigrants from Asian cultures to majority white countries.

In her essay 'Yellow' in *The Good Immigrant*, Vera Chok, a London-based actor and writer of Chinese descent, writes:

> What with the whitewashing of history and the darkness surrounding slavery and oppression, I don't feel as if I own, or am allowed to own, 'real suffering' because of the colour of my skin. Instead I bear a different kind of badge, one I'm supposed to be pleased about: 'model minority'.[1]

Chok is bravely inching her toe over the line that marks the boundary between those who can talk about oppression and those whose oppression is not considered significant enough to matter. In a world where African-Americans can be shot just for existing, and Syrian refugees are fleeing violence only to find borders closed to them in prosperous countries around the globe, it can seem trivial to find oneself preoccupied with the middle-class musings I am writing about here, but as Chok points out, a badge of any kind that is given to you without your consent is still a racial label, a definition that is grounded in stereotype.

Even when cast in a favourable light, the stereotype of Indian migrants as successful business owners plays into the idea of us as a homogenous group. We are not all shop owners, accountants or obsessive about cricket. The last thing I would want a benevolent white person to say to me is that my parents are the 'right kind of migrant' – the kind that subscribes to the inequality of a capitalist system and makes it work in their favour. Rather, as I've mentioned above, my parents' strong work ethic is a direct result of their upbringing in a developing country with a lack of opportunities.

This is also one of the reasons that the children of migrants often find themselves worlds apart from their parents when it comes to their careers and lifestyles. It's no surprise that despite the success of our parents' businesses, none of their four children has shown any desire to run small businesses of their own. If there's one thing that truly brings home the draining and all-consuming nature of running a business, it's watching your parents slog away at it for your entire childhood.

Of course, many immigrants work hard in whatever employment they can find (be it small business or otherwise), precisely so that their children won't have to do the same. My parents are an anomaly in that they are both highly educated and had professional careers before they emigrated – many of our Fijian-Indian family friends did not bring that experience with them to Australia. Some worked in factories or child-care. Their jobs involved shiftwork, paid little and required very hard work. A small business is also hard work but has the benefit of being self-driven and allowing the owner to develop an independent income stream. But if you had access to a western tertiary education and the Australian job market, would your first choice be to run a small business? Unless you have a passion for a particular type of business, I doubt it.

There's a reason why businesses set up by my generation are called 'start-ups' and their owners are 'entrepreneurs'. It's because small business has been rebranded as its owners have changed their perspective. For Generation Y, running a business is rarely just about making money. It's about 'following your bliss' or being a 'hustler' or the 'boss lady'. Or something. I doubt that when my parents were cleaning cheese grease out of the pans at the charcoal chicken shop they were following *their* bliss. But their hard work means that their children can. I can be a writer, as financially unviable as that is. My sisters can run their cake-decorating business alongside their 'real' jobs, because they want to do it for fun and not make it stressful. We can *choose* not to be stressed, a luxury never afforded to my parents.

As migrants and the children of migrants, the legacies we inherit are mixed – not just the good and the bad, but also what our parents want us to inherit and what they cannot prevent flowing down to their children.

Negative stereotypes about Indian migrants are something we have no control over, yet these same stereotypes can act as an unexpected uniting factor. I may have been embarrassed by my parents' businesses as a teenager, but these days I get a secret kick out of nodding along to an online meme sending up Indian parents, especially if it notes their supposed stinginess or business savvy. It makes me feel like I'm part of something bigger than just my family, and reminds me that a key way in which minority cultures escape prejudice is through reappropriating the terms or concepts that have been used to oppress them.

Besides, it's all in the way we frame these things. You say 'stingy', I say 'savvy'. You say 'cheap', I say 'thrifty'. You say 'cockroach', I say 'colonised culture creating change for generations to come, despite centuries of oppression'.

It's a mouthful, but it's true.

LIVING A HYPHENATED LIFE

A few years ago, I received an email from an honours student at a local university, asking me to participate in her research. Her thesis, she told me, was focusing on the way Fijian-Indian women in the diaspora of migrant Indian communities across the world became the custodians of culture in their new country.

My immediate reaction was to decline the invitation. I didn't feel I was qualified to participate. The term 'Fijian-Indian' in her email felt like a brand – she knew my background, and she felt certain enough of my connection to my cultural heritage to think that I could add something meaningful to her research. It made me feel pushed and pulled, caught in the constant tug of war that is my cultural identity. I am genetically Indian, I was born in Fiji, I'm a woman – I can understand why this student felt confident about approaching me for a research project that only required those details to determine my relevance.

But the facts alone don't make an identity. Despite my origins, I couldn't *feel* Fijian-Indian in a way that would make me a suitable person to interview on cultural custodianship. If anything, I have spent my life trying *not* to feel Fijian-Indian, desperate to prove that my cultural identity is as 'Australian' as that of my white friends who grew up in the same suburbs as me, attending the same schools, unravelling the same Australianness in their DNA that is in mine by virtue of citizenship. I didn't want to see myself as a custodian of a culture that I barely felt any connection with.

The desperation with which I rejected the Fijian-Indian label was a red flag, though. I'm desperate because I am grasping at an identity that requires the denial of my self. Without my Indianness and my Fijian birth, I would not exist. I certainly wouldn't be Australian, and I wouldn't have access to the experiences that helped me become the mishmash I am today. It's accepting that fact, which irrevocably separates me from my white Australian friends and admits an element of luck and chance and escape in my arrival in Australia, that makes me yearn to discard my heritage. I want an identity that can be captured in a single word, not a tangle of hyphens. I want my Australianness to be self-evident, not something that must be explained in response to the familiar question 'Where are you from?' – as if it's still so surprising for someone with brown skin to be 'from' Australia. And yet my yearning can't change the fact that I am harder to place than a single finger on a map. The fact that I *want* to change that is troubling in itself.

I agreed to participate in the honours project. I couldn't find a reasonable excuse not to, and it occurred to me that perhaps my lurking and hiding was exactly what made it impossible for me to reconcile with my Fijian-Indian origin. Instead, I turned to face it full on.

The label 'Fijian-Indian' (sometimes 'Indo-Fijian') is a perplexing one. Much like my own Australian identity, it was created to describe a cultural origin that exists as a result of human endeavour, not a natural existence. Indians wound up in Fiji through two primary avenues, which are conveniently demonstrated by the two sides of my own family history.

My mother's family's presence in Fiji stretches back generations, to when indentured labourers were first brought from India to Fiji by the British to work the sugar cane fields and support the burgeoning sugar cane industry. It was a time of uprootedness in both India and Fiji, with both countries coming to terms with their new identities under colonisation. There was political protest in Britain (at a time when there was a big push against slavery) at the use of native Fijians as farm workers, as this was a threat to their way of life, but no such concerns arose about the use of indentured labourers from India. I suppose the fact that there was a work arrangement, where labourers were paid (a pittance) – once they had worked off the cost of their journey – made the resemblance to slavery somewhat murkier and more acceptable.

All I know about my own family's experience of this journey is the tale told to me by my mother. The story goes that my great-great-grandfather was walking in a port town in India when someone approached him with the offer of a well-paid job. Having grown up in abject poverty, he agreed, boarded the ship in the dock and ended up in Fiji, where he had to work on a sugar cane farm to pay off the debt he'd accrued from the journey until he could eventually start to earn actual money. When the British started to leave Fiji in the 1960s and '70s, the white overseer of the farm where my ancestor laboured bequeathed the land and everything on it to him, as a show of respect for his work. This story, undoubtedly twisted from many retellings, is slightly rose-tinted. There is a seamlessness in the telling that suggests that my great-great-grandfather barely considered the offer before boarding the vessel that would take him – and ultimately generations of his descendants – away from his homeland. And the bestowal of property seems arbitrary – why him and not others? The systems by which success was measured in those days had the same desperate edges as my own identity quest. Having something as concrete as property to justify such an immense and irrevocable journey from home makes the sacrifice seem more worthwhile. In any case, the details of his story are lost forever, never committed to paper, staying a part of Britain's colonial history that is rarely given much airtime these days.

There is also an unspoken rule within the Fijian-Indian community (at least in the circles I grew up in) not to talk too deeply about these things. The country's bloody and tormented past, from colonisation to the numerous political coups that often led to riots, and the ability of displaced Indian communities to thrive regardless of their circumstances are somewhat taboo topics, and I imagine that my mother's family history has been blurred and massaged accordingly through generations.

One outcome of this legacy, though, so many years later, is that my mother isn't entirely certain where in India her family came from, other than knowing it was somewhere in the south. There is no family she has been able to look up, no reference to their past in India before they became embedded in a migrant culture in Fiji that is shackled to a postcolonial identity, and that is responsible for the displacement of native Fijians.

In contrast, my father's parents arrived in Fiji as economic migrants from Gujarat in the early 1930s, and made a life there, raising nine children. They joined the hordes of migrants from northern India who fled their homeland's poverty for the smaller population and greater opportunities in Fiji, despite it being so far away. My grandparents ran a small farm and a convenience store/petrol station in the rural town of Rakiraki. My father was born in Fiji, and grew up working the farm, playing in the fields and bathing in the nearby river.

As a second-generation migrant to Fiji, he too grappled with identity questions throughout his youth. He wanted to learn Gujarati, the dialect of his ancestors, but the local Hindi spoken in Fiji is a mix of formal Hindi and dialects. He yearned to visit his parents' villages in India, and to connect to his Indian heritage unfiltered through the sieve of Fiji, which created a unique strand of Indian culture that mingled practices from all regions of the country. These were connections he had to forge for himself as an adult, and that remain slightly out of his reach.

Frustratingly, Indians in India have a generalised disdain for Fijian-Indians, who are seen as uncouth and uncultured, an embarrassing subset of the Indian identity. Because of the boundaries between different cultures within India, and the strictness applied to ensuring that each subculture is retained in as pure a form as possible, the melding and merging of cultures in Fiji is dismissed as an abomination at worst, a mishap at best.

The irony of my father's cultural identity crisis isn't lost on me. His own desire not to lose his heritage was applied to his children in the form of a directive to hold our Indian traditions closer than any Australian ones we picked up along the way. Our religion as Muslims, our food, our gender roles, our language – these were all prioritised, even as we developed Australian accents that affected our pronunciation of Hindi, or travelled Australia and tried to quietly assimilate as migrants at a time when the very word 'migrant' was tainted.

As an adult, I now understand where his protectiveness came from. After battling to find and hold onto his own

Indian identity in Fiji, my father then faced the challenge of recreating it in Australia, and passing it on to his children. Watching your children morph into a different nationality from the one that you belong to and that they were born into must be a peculiar experience. But as a child, I was befuddled by the conflicting narratives I heard at home, at school and on the news. Where my parents wanted me to hold onto my Fijian-Indian identity, every other information source seemed to indicate that stripping off any outward signs of my difference was the best way to ensure my survival in the rapidly changing Australia of the 1990s.

We arrived in the country as part of the last wave of immigration under Paul Keating, before the rhetoric of Pauline Hanson and her One Nation party and John Howard's eleven-year reign as prime minister altered the public perspective on immigration. Keating was an ambassador of the 'Asian century', keen to build Australia's connections to its Asia-Pacific neighbours. Howard, on the other hand, wanted to lock Australia's borders down, while Hanson added fuel to the fire with her inflammatory racist dialogue.

I sometimes wonder whether our experiences of living in country Australia might have been different if Keating had remained in power. Unfortunately, we arrived just as the tide was turning, and there was a palpable distaste towards brown-skinned immigrants in the community we settled in.

We initially lived in the regional centre of Albury, where my father was employed as one of the first non-white engineers at an electricity company. School was a daily torment of racial slurs and bullying, and we had to drive more than four hours to find meat that was *halal* (slaughtered according to Islamic law). Hanson's face was spread across television screens and newspapers, and I remember feeling stressed when I heard her insisting that immigrants should 'go back to where they came from'. Terrified of being taken away from my new home, I pictured hiding under my bed or camping in a friend's garage when the authorities inevitably came to take us away.

This anxiety was no doubt exacerbated by the bullying I faced at school, and by how much we stood out in a town where there was only the occasional glimpse of brown amid the sea of white. It made sense, then, that the migrant population that did exist was a tight-knit one, and despite the other challenges, we forged a community that swiftly became central to our lives. A local church allowed us to use their hall for our prayer meetings and Islamic school, and all the women, whether Bosnian, Pakistani, Malaysian or Fijian-Indian, shared the cooking of sweets for Eid and the catering of our regular barbecues. Following our multi-generational history of migration, my family had arrived in yet another country and founded a new version of ourselves, now mingling the many cultures of our friends with our own traditions. It was one of the richest, most enjoyable chapters of our lives, even with the more systemic challenges.

In many ways, our first six years in Australia strengthened our own relationships, and the identities of my parents. With only the six of us to really rely on, our family was incredibly close. We had in-jokes and games that no one else understood, and an unflinching loyalty that still exists today. My parents had to let go of chunks of their identity in the move – my mother was a high-school teacher in Fiji but, unsure of teaching in this new culture, she opted out of the profession in Australia. Instead, she got a job at Franklins supermarkets, first packing shelves, and eventually as a stock controller. My heart thumps with admiration for her when I think of this now – a woman in her early thirties, giving up the relatively prestigious role of a teacher in Fiji to be a supermarket worker in a foreign country where people's expectations in the workplace are completely different. This could have been a difficult time for Mum, but instead she made lifelong friends, and created a community through work that opened us up to picnic days and new 'aunts' and 'uncles' to replace those we had left in Fiji. Similarly, my father didn't wait to reconstruct his own networks. He made friends, took up golf, played squash with workmates and built our house from scratch with a few other men.

As I've described, my parents are the epitome of hard-working 'model' migrants. They have gone from brushing the edges of the middle class in Fiji to being comfortably wealthy in Australia, through grit and hard work. This is the migrant narrative that predominantly white capitalist societies accept – one of economic productivity and quiet achievement, where migrants are given little and take even less, but are able to spin gold from the straw offered to them by their adopted country. This is contrasted to the caricature of 'bad migrants' spouted by right-wing governments the world over – the scrounging alien who expects their new home to provide for them, draining the system – or, worse, who walks into jobs taken from deserving nationals.

Mainstream culture expects immigrants to be grateful for the opportunities Australia has granted them, and to contribute to the economy without expecting anything in return. Being 'good' immigrants in this way doesn't protect us from racism and ridicule. The number of times I have seen older white people roll their eyes when we arrive at a restaurant, or had checkout staff talk to my mother in a slow, loud voice, as if her hijab prevents her from hearing, are too many to count.

When I reflect on how alienating that early time in Australia must have been, I realise it is no wonder that my parents cling to their Fijian-Indian identities with such zeal. Their selfhood is built on their culture, which is firmly rooted in Fiji and in India, in that order. They manage the balance of their Indian heritage and the new traditions that have developed over the decades of Indian inhabitation of Fiji, like cooking food in a *lovo* pit, and the different sweets, curries and even clothing styles that have evolved there. They have managed to maintain both identities without the dissonance I feel. In this, they are true custodians of culture. There are no traditions that they have allowed to lapse. For Eid, we made our own vermicelli, sometimes spending weekends stretching out the fine spaghetti-like pastry on sheets all over the porch. We watched Bollywood classics, and played the much-loved carrom board game. We learned Hindi insults, and when I was a child my father sang me to sleep with Indian lullabies every night without fail.

Their dedication was fundamental to our upbringing. Yet while my siblings seemed to adapt and acclimatise to the dual cultural forces in our lives, between school and home, with ease, I still held myself apart. I was unable to see the pockets of inclusion in our lives; instead, I was focused – always – on the differences. The legacy that brought me to Australia, and my seminal early years in Albury, had made impressions on me, but not necessarily the ones my parents hoped for. I was becoming untethered from what made me and searching for a hook into the teeming waves of Australian culture that seethed around me but somehow kept slipping through my grasp.

As a teenager, I was particularly prone to the sullen moodiness often associated with adolescence. If my father said 'good morning' to me while I was eating breakfast, I often yelled at him to 'just leave me alone', before storming to my bedroom, while my parents gave each other the look that said, 'Zoya's sulking . . . *again*.' If I caught a hint of mockery from my siblings, it would spark a fit of the nobody-understands-mes.

Few occasions brought out this terrible teenage side more strongly than daytrips to go shopping in the Indian streets of

Liverpool in western Sydney. Looking back, I'm as puzzled by my negativity as my mother was then. I mean, a road trip with my mum and sisters to Sydney, where we shopped for clothes and delicious Indian *mithai*, and often gossiped and listened to Bollywood music along the way – what's not to love? But teenage Zoya, despite secretly enjoying the changing-room shenanigans and hanging out with her cool older sisters and far-too-nice mother, still felt as if the whole Indian fashion thing was holding her back from her true fashion identity (vaguely goth, vaguely alternative, no sequins in sight).

We would spend hours walking up and down the main drag of Indian shops, visiting stores like Roop Darshan's and Roshan's Fashions. Mannequins hung from hooks along the tops of the walls, demonstrating the latest fashions in *salwar kameez* and *ghagra cholis*. Despite myself, I yearned to wear the sequined tunics and trousers with the confidence and grace of a Bollywood heroine. Many of my childhood daydreams had revolved around performing Bollywood-style dances on a grassy knoll in Europe (often the setting of Bollywood musical sequences), dressed head to toe in the kind of modest-yet-sultry outfit that was favoured at the time, with my partner, Salman Khan, one of the big names of the day. Now, though, I wanted both to throw off the constraints of Indian culture, and the restraint it demands of women, and to own it, to immerse myself in it. This push–pull in my identity has been a constant in my life. I wanted to take part in both halves of my cultural upbringing – the Australian and the Fijian-Indian – but neither wanted to muddy the waters of its essence with the other.

To be 'cool' as a teenager, I needed to be counterculture, and the counterculture that interested me in the early 2000s was embodied by Gwen Stefani and the gothic Lolita fashion scene, not bravely wearing my heritage on my sleeve and owning my Indianness. The few times I did try to bring the two together, the results didn't feel right. I once wore a *kameez* top over flared jeans to a school mufti day, and immediately felt dowdy next to my friends in their denim shorts and tank tops. I stood out, but not in the way I wanted.

These daytrips to Sydney encapsulated this unspoken conflict between the two halves of my self. I was sullen and cynical (channelling Daria and the *Gilmore Girls*' Lane Kim), but sometimes surreptitiously leaned forward to finger the soft fabric of a *dupatta*, and secretly enjoyed the latest Bollywood hits playing on the shops' TV screens. Our days were jam-packed. The sales assistants pulled out different combinations, packed in crackly plastic cases, and arrayed them on the wide counters in front of us. My sisters and I tried on a range of outfits, either for an upcoming wedding or just to expand our wardrobes before we went to Fiji. Comments and sales talk flew in rapid-fire Hindi. We also bought bangles and other jewellery, and occasionally we'd go to a Bollywood music and DVD store to pick up the latest releases from India.

As I write this, I am overcome with a surge of nostalgia for those days spent immersed in our culture. My life now is steeped in whiteness, my closet almost entirely bereft of Indian outfits, other than the one my mother buys me every year for Eid. At some point, around the time I graduated from high school, I went from only occasionally wearing Indian clothes to not wearing them at all. The items gradually disappeared from my wardrobe. Maybe I added one or two *kameez* at a time to my charity donations bag during a clothing cull, or left hangers of saris at my parents' house when I moved out. I might have given bags of clothes to my cousins when they visited. Gradually, bit by bit, I removed every non-western item of clothing from my wardrobe, and now there is no space for them. The shelves and racks are crammed with jeans and jackets and floral dresses. My days of trying on the latest Indian fashions with my sisters were behind me, and try as I might, I couldn't find a path back to them.

At the time, though, despite the enjoyment every teenage girl takes in buying new clothes, I would trail behind my family with a dim sense of embarrassment when we passed white people, aware of how different we must appear. There was an independent record store in Liverpool, and I begged Mum to let me duck in while they continued to a cafe for lunch. As I rifled through old records looking for a copy of Joy Division's *Closer* and albums from bands like The Smiths, it was almost as if I was performing a rite of identity for the benefit of the middle-aged white shop owner. My record choices and consciously cool stance at the shelves were meant to indicate that I might *look* like the Indians crowding the pavement outside, but I wasn't really like them – I was more like him.

There is a photo from my year ten formal, which was held at the fanciest hotel in town. My parents always allowed us to go to the school formal but not the after-party, which was usually held at someone's house or a local club, and was more likely to include underage drinking and flirtation than the formal sit-down dinner. In the photo, I am standing with five of my close friends. It's a sunny evening, and the cool green backdrop of the hotel garden sets off the rainbow colours of our clothes. My friends are in short cocktail dresses, their hair carefully arranged. I am wearing a bronze-coloured *ghagra choli* with a black mesh overlay and intricate beading. I remember loving the outfit when I saw it in Liverpool, but when the night of the formal arrived I felt uncomfortably conspicuous, the token ethnic. My skirt reaches to my ankles, and the top is not fitted enough to give any sense of my waist or the curves of my hips. It is sparkly, but it is not stunning.

I'm smiling, but there is a reticence in my smile, a holding in that makes the present me clench a little in my gut. I remember that night. I remember standing against the curtains in the ballroom, unwilling to even attempt to dance (the refrain in my head reminding me that dancing is *haram*, forbidden). I remember thinking how grown-up everyone looked. I remember the piercing, bittersweet sense of transience as I thought of our impending graduation. At sixteen I was so certain that these moments were a small glimpse into a life I probably wouldn't lead – an Indian husband, or at least the stereotype of one that lived in my mind, wouldn't want to twirl around to the '90s pop songs playing through the venue's speakers. A married woman wouldn't go to gigs, or experiment with her hairstyle, or study Romantic poets at university as my friends would be doing in the coming years. Even if I could do all of these things, I would never have the freedom to reinvent myself and try new things the way my friends would. If I was married, fundamental parts of my identity would be tethered to my husband's, such as where I lived or the work I did. I couldn't quit university and move to Paris on a whim, or live on a pittance and experience the life of a struggling artist. My friends had control over their futures, which stretched out ahead of them. I was a traveller where they were residents. My difference was unavoidable, literally clinging to me and marking me out from my friends and peers. My *ghagra* wrapped around me, and tethered me to my Indianness. I wanted badly to escape it, and I spent the following years of young adulthood doing my utmost to discard Indian traditions so I might better fit the vision I had of an exciting life – a vision that had no hint of cultural difference from my white Australian peers.

What I didn't realise at the time is that cultural identity isn't elastic – stretching to fit me, and closing behind me to cover the gap, ready for when I next attempt to try it on. I had fallen into the trap of assuming that the way I saw cultural identity practised around me, as all or nothing, Indian *or*

Australian, was the only way it could work. I didn't understand that I could strike out with a new goal, create space for both cultures in my life. In so doing I could pave the way for the next generation, and also dispel some of the fears my parents and their generation had about the potential negative influence of Australian culture on their children.

By discarding aspects of my Fijian-Indian heritage, I risked losing them forever. If I wanted to wear Indian clothes now, it would be a far bigger endeavour than simply ordering a sari online. I don't accompany my mother and sisters on their Indian shopping expeditions anymore – they don't often mention when they're planning a trip, and I can't blame them for assuming I wouldn't be interested in joining them. I think Mum sometimes feels awkward when she buys me my annual Eid outfit, as if I might throw a tantrum, or refuse to accept it – this breaks my heart. I have created my own cage, and I struggle to see a way out of it now. I know that there are ways for me to reconnect with these aspects of Indian culture, but it feels like such an insurmountable task to chip through the walls I've built around myself.

My experience is very different from that of my sisters. A glance at their Facebook pages shows that they can flit easily between their two worlds, because they have always kept the door between them open. It is a knack I never thought I needed, until it started feeling like it was too late.

This disconnect from my Fijian-Indian self occurred not in one decisive moment but as a series of erosions. I remember sometimes feeling an overwhelming sense of dissonance, such as when I was making roti at home with my sisters, realising that this side of my identity had little connection to my sense of self when I was with my friends, giggling about how cute Legolas was in *The Lord of the Rings*. I was one person, but my self was divided. The way I behaved in 'Indian' settings was markedly different from how I was at school or with my friends. My outspokenness, my feminism, my creativity were all things that I held apart from Indian gatherings and our network of Muslim friends. This was not because I was expected to, but because I erroneously assumed no one would be interested in my thoughts on global politics or the novel I was writing after school.

I now know how stupid this was. One of the best spoken-word artists and playwrights to come out of Canberra is a young Muslim woman I grew up with, one year younger than me. She is a feminist, wildly creative and genuinely lovely – but during our many years of attending the same events, we never connected, and I'm certain that wasn't her fault. Of course, my assumption that the Fijian-Indian and other Muslim people we knew would be bored by my interests was partly symptomatic of my moody adolescent phase. But it was also an enactment of my constant feelings of cultural alienation – I just wasn't aware that I was (at least partly) doing this to myself.

Seeing it this way makes me realise that schools and other community resources have never found a way to meaningfully engage with young migrants. I created these walls because I couldn't see another way to fit in. If I had been given the tools to navigate this cultural difference, and if my white friends were also better schooled in inclusion, perhaps things would have been different. But Australia's approach to multiculturalism often takes the form of a benevolent othering. Every multicultural festival centred on food and dance, every time a teacher expected me to bring in an Indian artefact for show and tell, every time a parent called me 'the nice Indian girl' when describing me to another parent at a party – these moments all created a larger pattern of focusing only on my difference, which made me want to redefine myself entirely.

I was never told that I could be a goth *and* be Indian. Or that I could love *Gilmore Girls* and watch Bollywood movies. Or that wearing a *salwar kameez* one day wouldn't prevent me from wearing a western-style skirt and top the next. I think my parents implied these things, but because we never really addressed cultural difference head on, I was mostly left to construct my identity myself, which felt like a constant battle between Fijian-Indian and Australian norms.

Writing it down, those terms seem archaic in today's more globalised world. Now it seems obvious that the boundaries between cultures are largely imagined – it is possible to blend cultural influences without having to pledge allegiance to all or nothing of any particular culture. But when I was in high school, cultural education was limited by geographic location and access to sources of information. We still had dial-up internet, and social media didn't exist. We could chat on MSN, and I had a LiveJournal and a fanfiction.net account (the usernames for which I will take to my grave), but I accessed culture largely through real-life experiences.

Despite having a loving home, and a wide choice of activities through my family, I always wanted what I couldn't have. I wanted the Hollywood movies and the Blue Light discos at the local youth centre; I wanted to go to all-ages shows and attend the school socials where everyone danced to the latest music. I wanted the pink streaks in my hair and the nail polish that I wasn't allowed to wear until I was older because it was *haram*. Most of all, I desperately wanted everyone else to see me as more 'Australian' than not, because somewhere along the way my mild resentment at the restrictions of my culture had been replaced by a low-level self-hatred that I now know is common among young first-generation migrants.

The seed of this self-hatred is planted by the unwillingness of mainstream Australian society to see cultural diversity as anything other than a burden. After all, it wasn't until 2011 that *Neighbours* featured a non-white family on Ramsay Street, a decision that met with so much hostility that it attracted international media attention. If I wanted to be fully included in what I saw as Australian culture, I would have to carve out that space for myself, always *despite* my obvious non-whiteness. I spent years feeling as though I was slowly constructing a full-body mask, and that if I just made it convincing enough, I'd finally be able to pass as an 'Australian'. I thought that maybe if I sounded more Australian, looked and acted more Australian, my skin colour would become irrelevant and I could finally fly under the radar.

This radar was not just about the way white people homed in on my difference, forcing me to account again and again for where I was 'from'. (The word 'from' in this context has always puzzled me. It implies movement, progress of some sort. Really, they are asking, 'What are you made of?') It was also about wanting to confirm for myself, finally, that I *could* have the same experiences as my friends – that I could be unconflicted in my pursuit of art, music and writing. That my cultural background would be a part of the tapestry of my being – not the whole tapestry, including the hooks and threads that keep it bound to the wall.

So I relished my smooth Aussie accent, pleased when people couldn't tell over the phone whether I was white or brown, and I prided myself on doing all the 'Aussie' things I could think of – going swimming at beaches, attending music festivals – instead of watching Bollywood movies, playing Indian board games and learning how to make perfect roti. As well as weeding out the Indian clothes from my wardrobe, I steered clear of any jewellery that looked 'ethnic', and smoothed my wild Indian curls into a sleek, straight bob.

The straightening of my hair was something I always dismissed when asked about it. Frequently, friends and well-meaning colleagues would ask me why I didn't wear my hair curly anymore. 'You're so lucky to have such nice curls,' they would say. 'You should wear your hair curly more often.' I would explain it away as a matter of convenience – straight hair was easier to maintain, and I didn't have to wash it every day as I did when it was curly. I said this so often that I almost began to believe it myself. Only recently, when reading a passage from Durga Chew-Bose's essay 'D As In', from her collection *Too Much and Not the Mood*, did I have a moment of sharp, gut-churning recognition. Chew-Bose is a Canadian-Indian writer who has beautifully explored the complexity of racial identity when living between two cultures, and in this essay she writes: 'Nothing will make you fit in less than trying, constantly, to fit in: portioning your name, straightening your hair . . .'[2] It was the first time I had read someone from a somewhat similar background to mine summarising exactly what I have felt but never been able to articulate.

In those words, I recognised my own unspoken need to smooth out the edges of my difference, to make myself more acceptable to the white gaze. I remember clearly when I decided to start straightening my hair. It was in my first year of university, and one of my close male friends from high school had met a new crowd of alternative, arty friends. All of them, men and women, were fascinated by a girl in the group who took edgy photographs and always looked a bit fragile. She had dark brown hair, cut asymmetrically, falling in lush, glossy waves around her face. I observed how everyone gazed at her with different shades of adoration, and I yearned to be like her. That week, I cut my long curly hair and started straightening it daily. And people really did treat me differently, I felt. Perhaps it was self-deception, but it seemed that looks lingered longer, smiles were friendlier – sometimes people I'd gone to school with didn't even recognise me. It made me feel pretty and accepted; conversely, I felt ugly and too 'ethnic-looking' when my hair was curly.

Of course, my experience is the tip of the iceberg when it comes to hair in race politics. The significance of hair for African-American women, and the way it can be a site for postcolonial racism, is something I only really became aware of when I read Chimamanda Ngozi Adichie's 2013 novel *Americanah*. The main character, a young Nigerian woman named Ifemelu, struggles with her own African appearance when she moves to America, noting how African-American women tame their hair with chemical relaxers and weaves and extensions. However, as she begins to forge a new identity in America, her hair becomes Ifemelu's weapon against this insidious westernisation of African women – eventually she eschews all attempts at taming it and wears it in an afro, despite the renewed challenges she faces when she looks more 'jungle', as one man describes it. But when her friend Wambui first urges Ifemelu to discard relaxing her hair for a natural afro, Ifemelu is resistant. Wambui says, 'Relaxing your hair is like being in a prison. You're caged in. Your hair rules you . . .'[3]

Reading this passage was a small revelation at the time, a moment of proof that my own struggles weren't just vanity, they were encouraged and enforced by society. I reflected on my life since I'd started straightening my hair. I was constantly petrified of rain, in case my hair went frizzy. I only exercised alone, so I could wash my hair, dry it and straighten it again afterwards without friends seeing my sweaty hair start to curl. When I first started seeing Chris, I avoided having a shower at his house when I needed to wash my hair, because I thought he wouldn't find me attractive with curly hair. To this day, I feel less attractive, too *other*, when my hair is curly. Combined with my western clothing, my accent, the practised 'fuck off' expression that I wear in public, when I have straight hair I feel I have some armour against the questioning and the racial othering. Without all of this, I am a target, and not the master of my own destiny.

In my second year of university, just as I was carefully concealing any outwardly Indian parts of my personality, I started noticing that other Indian-Australian women around me were fully embracing their cultural identity. And they were considered extremely cool for doing so.

Girls came to uni wearing *kurti* tops over jeans in an effortless blending of cultures that suggested an ease with their identity I was sorely lacking. The ball held annually by the South Asian Students' Society was always sold out; a Bollywood-style musical performed to packed audiences; and my Instagram feed started regularly featuring friends posting proudly about visiting their temple/mosque, or dancing at their cousin's Hindu wedding. Everything I had tried to conceal was being vibrantly celebrated by my peers, and not a single person was mocking them for it.

My feeling of not belonging was suddenly reversed – now, even while I was more accepted as an Australian, I felt as if my Indian identity was lacking. Watching other young Australians bridging the gap between their two cultures and finding an identity that was multifaceted and complex made me realise that I had lost something by trying to simplify my own identity to fit in. I realised that my constant feeling of wrongfootedness, which makes me unsure how to proceed in social situations where another Indian is present, or feel awkward when a white friend asks for Bollywood recommendations (they probably know more about current Bollywood movies than I do), is a result of self-induced alienation from the cultures that made me. For other young women, especially those who had culturally diverse close friends, this hadn't been such an either/or journey.

How does belonging exist within the space between two different cultures? It had never occurred to me to see my cultural difference as something that could be 'cool', a way to find friends and a community within broader Australian society. I always saw it as something that set me apart from my peers.

Again, my sisters were far ahead of me in this regard. Zaheeda has never flinched from acknowledging her cultural heritage. She was proud to have a traditional marriage in Fiji, and she's as happy listening to Bollywood tracks while driving as she is yelling the lyrics to a Maroon 5 song. Meanwhile, Zakia has a Facebook page for the henna art she does for Indian women's weddings. Her bedroom is decorated with photos and memorabilia from our trips to Fiji, and she used to wear Indian outfits to school mufti days with pride.

So why did I struggle so much? Was it just because I'm the youngest and have no real memories of living in Fiji? Or is it because I've always been so desperately afraid of standing out that I created this cultural prison for myself? If the latter, how did I drift so far from the core of who I am? It is hard for me to admit the shame and embarrassment I have internalised for so many years, because the act of dissociation is so at odds with the person I aim to be. I want to be proud of my heritage, of my difference, to ignore the detracting voices of a homogenised white culture. But instead I am weak, driven to change myself to fit in with the expectations of others. This is something I hate to see in myself, and something I can't trace back to any one moment – instead, it has seeped into me over years.

Now, as I face the prospect of always being on the outside of my culture looking in, a new set of anxieties is emerging. Whenever I am with a group of Indian-Australians, I feel that I stick out like a sore thumb. I worry that if I have to respond to someone in Hindi they will notice how bad my accent is. I hate answering questions about Indian culture from well-meaning colleagues or friends in case I get it wrong, and

I constantly feel that other Indians are judging me for what I wear, or say, or do. I know that these insecurities are in large part internally driven, but the process of becoming Australian has scoured away at my Fijian-Indian origins, and now I find it difficult to imagine ever really owning either identity.

The greater the distance between my childhood experience and my current life, the fuzzier and more opaque my understanding of Indian culture becomes. My grasp of Hindi is slipping, my pronunciation becoming more and more 'Aussie'. When I speak to my grandmother on the phone, I stumble over my words while she struggles to understand me. I seldom eat traditional food, and the little things I grew up assuming I would always be able to do – making round roti, or folding samosas into perfect triangles – now seem alien to me. Once, I used to stand at the stove with my sisters in a production line – one kneading the dough, the other rolling it out, and me cooking the roti on a flat, oil-free pan, the heat from the stove making my hair curl. But now I can't remember the feeling of the pan in my hand, or the dough under my fingers.

Now that I live out of home, I am often not around when the rest of my family is engaging in our traditions or cultural days. This is partly a result of my 'busy schedule', but it is also self-preservation, my desire to avoid confronting how far I have drifted, by drifting even further. My only connections to my culture are memories of the past, and the occasional outing with my mother to the local Indian grocery store. I worry that the link to my Indian heritage is reliant on my parents being alive, and that in years to come I'll struggle to remember the culture that ultimately made me.

When I participated in the honours project, I felt like an imposter. Can I even call myself a Fijian-Indian? Do I have the right to speak on behalf of the cultural group? I pushed through these feelings to do the interview, but when the finished thesis was sent to me, months later, I was struck by the results. I was one of the only women interviewed who had anything negative to say about being Fijian-Indian in Australia. While other women spoke of engaging with their culture and being proud of their heritage, my sense of loneliness and unbelonging haunted my interview. Many women said that they felt happiest in traditional clothing, wearing their identity as a badge of honour, while I admitted to feeling constricted by Indian clothes, always feeling like an outsider. Other women wrote about the pleasure they took in cooking Fijian-Indian food, or visiting Fiji with their families, but I hadn't visited Fiji with my family for years, and since becoming an adult I had barely connected with family members there.

Reading the results, I felt sad and wistful. Sad that I had pushed myself so far away from the current of Indian culture that I hadn't even realised how much I had drifted. Wistful for the confidence and warmth that emerged in the other women's interviews. On the other hand, it was a little comforting to realise that these other women – who also had jobs and friends, and exciting lives – felt no awkwardness or shame about our culture. For them, being Fijian-Indian was a source of pride, and the uniqueness of our culture was something to be celebrated.

Part of breaking down racial barriers and stereotypes is acknowledging that the idea of an 'Indian-Australian' may be as meaningless as the idea of an 'Australian', in the sense that neither of those terms can ever encapsulate the diversity of voices, experiences and values held by the groups of people they describe. In Fiji, I am Fijian-Indian. In India, I am Australian, Fijian, Gujarati. In Australia, I am Fijian and Indian, as well as being a Canberran. Our world is becoming smaller, and there is so much fluidity and movement that using racial terms to describe identity is becoming more and more abstract.

For now, I continue to feel a sense of displacement. I am hopeful that this will eventually ease, and that a path will emerge where my cultural identities have come together into a stronger sense of self. I am going to start reading about Indian and Fijian history, and I want to collect the stories of my family through the generations so I can fully understand where we have come from. I have been gradually building back up my Indian wardrobe, a task my mother has been more than happy to help with. And I force myself to speak to my nieces and nephew in Hindi as much as possible, to keep the language active in my mind.

I have also started writing down my mother's recipes for my favourite Fijian-Indian foods, recording her secret spice combinations so that I don't have to worry that they'll be lost when she is gone. When I stand with her in the kitchen, steam and smoke from frying onions filling the air, along with the intense aroma of spices – turmeric, garam masala, chilli – I can almost feel a connection again. I write it all down, and it makes me feel that there is a permanence to my culture, as mixed as it is, that can't be lost as easily as I might fear. It lives on inside me, through the memories that don't fade entirely, and through the footprints of taste, scent and sound – the way that my heart speeds up when I hear the jangle of a favourite old Bollywood song, or taste the *aloo channa* my mother makes with tinned tomatoes.

I might struggle to hold onto my culture in all the ways I want to, but I now know it's there for me to grasp when I'm ready.

MONEY CAN'T BUY HARMONY

When I was fourteen, I travelled with a group of culturally diverse teenagers on a government-funded bus tour around rural New South Wales, spreading the message of cultural harmony. There were Indians, Asians, Somalis, a Ghanaian, Pacific Islanders, a Russian, an Iranian filmmaker hired to document the trip, two young women who were our tutors on the trip, and two older men (one white, one black) who were the public servants in charge of the whole show.

We travelled to a number of towns and visited high schools and primary schools, performing traditional dances and sharing our visions for a racism-free Australia. Then we would meet with local politicians, before going to the budget hotel where we were staying that night and pretending to do homework.

If you're thinking this sounds like a bizarre experience, you would be right. In fact, it was probably even more bizarre than you're imagining.

Picture this: it's a hot spring day in 2004, and the students of Moruya High School on the south coast are being dragged into their school hall for a 'special assembly'. The 'special' part of the assembly is, essentially, us – a motley crew of young people, of various levels of coolness, brought together to demonstrate how not-scary we are, despite our 'different' skin colours and/or accents.

First, a young Indian woman (not me) performs a traditional dance, in a bright-orange sparkly sari. The Russian boy recites poetry about his homeland, and the Ghanaian performs some hip-hop dancing. Then there's me – using the only skill I have to deliver an 'inspiring' speech about living with racism in Australia. The teenagers stare at us impassively. A group of girls giggle a little, and on stage we all shuffle uncomfortably. Three girls from the Pacific Islands appear in matching outfits and perform a traditional dance, their bodies swaying in mesmerising unison. Finally, a teacher comes out and asks the assembled school if there are any questions (invariably there aren't), and everyone claps reluctantly before we leave.

Repeat this about fifteen times.

Today, saturated as our culture is with reality TV shows depicting everything from poverty porn to regular porn, this premise could actually be successful as entertainment, if they stopped pretending there was some measurable result we were working towards. In reality, I felt a general sense of apathy from each audience, and our own unease upon realising that we were usually the only non-white people in the building. In one school there was a single Vietnamese-Australian boy, who visibly shrank down in his seat as we performed, as if he wanted to make it clear that he wasn't associated with this ragtag mob of weirdos who all happened to not be 'Aussie'.

Before we left on the tour, though, while we were still rehearsing in Canberra, I had felt energised, excited to be involved with something that gave me weeks off school and time away from home. And I really did feel we could change things by 'normalising' our differences. Back then, I saw difference as something to be explained, acclimatised to. I wanted to excuse my difference – instead, the tour amplified it.

The Harmony Ambassador tour was dreamed into existence by a few middle-aged bureaucrats in the Australian Capital Territory government, some of whom were white. The basic premise was to showcase how great people of colour (POC) can be, and, through entertainment and storytelling, bridge the divide between young people in rural and regional towns (areas assumed to have the lowest exposure to multiculturalism) and young POC, with the goal of ending racism. Or something.

The concept isn't that different from the theory of primary prevention in public health campaigns – basically, that if you can address something at its root before it becomes a problem, you can stop it growing into a monster. So, get kids to stop being racist and hopefully we can breed out the racist adults in time. A noble objective, for sure.

However, in execution it all felt a bit . . . slapdash. This could have been partly because I wasn't privy to the organisational efforts behind the scenes, but I do remember a lot of afternoon rehearsals in a conference room at the organisers' offices, where there was very little briefing on key messaging and expected outcomes, and a lot of time just looking on as Amy from Ghana practised twerking while watching her reflection in a window.

The key flaw in the design, from my perspective in hindsight, was that the program based its strategy on the false premise that racism results from a lack of education or awareness, as opposed to being the enactment of the innate human need to create in-groups and out-groups. Yes, educating children about diversity and inclusion is important, but without also addressing some of the other causes of the in-group/out-group mentality, including economic inequality, it's unlikely we can end racism in its entirety.

The bureaucrats thought that putting us in front of groups of unwilling young people in small towns up and down New South Wales would assuage their anxiety about POC and reassure them that we really weren't that different from them – as if racism were caused by a simple misunderstanding, where the racist confuses a brown person for a mythical monster and just needs to be shown that they are in fact human too. But racism, in my experience, does not always come from a lack of awareness or understanding. Racists aren't simply 'stupid' or misinformed. Generally, racists are people acting from a sense of injustice or frustration, and the scapegoat they have chosen is the group with the least similarity to them – in this case, immigrants. When it comes to young people, my guess is that their racism stems from their family's racism, and then is reinforced by their peer groups. Yes, you can change these attitudes over time through education, but it would require a multi-pronged approach aimed at all age groups, and would have to be combined with addressing some of the structural causes, such as poverty, isolation in rural communities, and representations of diversity in media.

The towns we visited during the Harmony Ambassador tour were different in size but often shared a general sense of dreariness, the main streets inevitably a bit rundown. Many coastal towns in New South Wales are built on closed economies, meaning there is one main source of jobs and income, maybe a factory or a particular farmed produce – something that relies on a tangible product or goods and can easily be threatened by broader factors. If your economy relies on a good grain-growing season and you have a drought, the negative impact of this trickles down to everyone in town. And the tightness of their economies means that these towns often have a fairly static population, with change easily marked. For small communities such as these, immigration is often seen as a destabiliser, and a threat to the limited number of employment opportunities on offer.

Years later, at the age of 22, I visited similar towns in different states as a member of the federal government's Social Inclusion Board. I had been selected for the board presumably to provide a 'youth' perspective, but the meetings often left me feeling stressed and unsure of myself, especially as we reported to the prime minister, and everyone else on the board was very prominent in their field. I was a young nobody who had won some volunteering awards as a teenager and gained a small profile in Canberra. I didn't feel particularly qualified to provide policy advice to the leader of the country, but I did value the chance to learn from everyone else on the board. Our objective was to look at factors that caused or heightened social isolation in the areas of Australia with the most disadvantage, and we travelled across the country to see these places in person. With each visit, I saw that behind the surfer beaches and poky high streets were high rates of generational unemployment, apathetic teenagers described as 'delinquents', and such a small number of part-time or casual jobs available to young people that they had very little in the way of personal income with which to pursue their own interests and hobbies.

I can imagine how claustrophobic it might feel to grow up in a small community, and also how loyal and connected you would feel to those with mirrored experiences. It's easy to extrapolate how shared racial prejudice could further solidify the connections within the white population in the town and help to create a sense of shared identity. Obviously #NotAllSmallTowns, et cetera – I'm not implying that every town outside of a major city is automatically racist – but the conditions for racism to grow are certainly easier to see.

The organisers of the Harmony Ambassador tour had been operating on the basis that cultural change was the primary solution to racism, when in fact top-down cultural change is usually fleeting without complementary structural change. Having a stranger perform their 'traditional' dance in front of an audience of truculent teenagers is unlikely to change the outcomes for the one or two non-white kids at the school. If there's no attempt to create new employment opportunities, to give young people in rural or regional areas the chance to get some work experience, and to generally connect Australians more despite the barriers of geographic distance, I don't see any change sticking.

Crucially, by ignoring the potential class barrier the tour could highlight, the organisers were creating an even greater divide between the audiences and our narratives. The young people sullenly observing as we paraded our difference were likely to feel only more alienated by my speech outlining the difficulties I experienced as a POC from a relatively affluent background, when they may have been experiencing degrees of economic disadvantage, unstable employment for their parents, and small chance of ever getting out.

How can you attempt to humanise one group without also viewing the opposite group through the same lens? There appeared to be very little effort by the organisers to engage our audience beyond seeing them as passive receivers of the messages we were imparting. The fact that the tour was created and delivered by public servants operating from an upper-middle-class perspective only increased this gap in understanding.

Canberra as a community (I can say this, having lived there most of my life) is largely detached from economic inequality. Disadvantage definitely exists in the Australian Capital Territory, but on average Canberrans have the highest salaries in Australia, and the city-state has good health and education services. Basically, when most of us are sitting in our ivory towers sipping lattes, it's easy to forget about the homeless guy on the corner selling *The Big Issue*. Importantly, factors such as income status, social circles and self-affirmation have an impact on racial attitudes: people who are better-off financially are usually more inclined to be progressive, and vice versa.

In his essay published in *Meanjin* 'In Defence of the Bad, White Working Class', Australian writer Shannon Burns compares his own attitudes to immigrants to those of his parents. Describing his parents as 'underemployed anglo-Australians', Burns delves more deeply into the issue of racism among the working class than most liberal progressives are willing to do. As he writes, 'I confess that if a well-dressed, university-educated middle-class person of any gender or ethnicity so much as hinted at my "white privilege" . . . I'd have taken special pleasure in voting for their nightmare.'[4] Burns is implying that while the affluent educated youth in cities like Canberra can afford to sit around casting judgement on those less well-off than them for not being as ideologically progressive, the inability of this mainstream liberal approach to see the inequalities experienced by the majority white working class creates a sort of impulse to fulfil the stereotypes of that population as being prejudiced and small-minded. #NotAllWhitePeople are racist, and not all racism comes from a genuine hatred of cultural difference – it's important when trying to address the issue not to create 'us versus them' systems where all racists are seen as baddies who just hate people of colour without any reason, and all left-wing not-racist people are morally superior. Because until we understand why people are driven to racist attitudes and see them as people rather than just symbols of an ideology, we can't change anything.

I imagine that many of the teenagers who sat with their arms crossed, tapping their feet impatiently as I described in passionate tones what it feels like as a POC to be constantly asked where you're 'from', were feeling at least a small amount of scorn. If that was my single biggest problem, the one I chose to present to them in the five minutes allocated to me to change their attitudes to racial equality, it was hardly rousing. Yes, those small acts of prejudice combine into a larger framework of erasure and devaluing of identity that can have a tangible impact on the lives of POC. But it would be naive to assume that racism springs entirely out of irrational hatred and stereotyping, instead of a wrongful linking of negative experiences with a scapegoat.

In his essay, Burns goes on to describe the shame he felt at his parents' racism, which was starkly different from his own attitudes. He went to school with majority non-white students, and his peer group was largely made up of Vietnamese and Chinese Australians. But his parents, without a similar engagement and immersion, blamed the new immigrant population for many of the problems of the neighbourhood. In turn, the Asian community viewed their white working-class neighbours with distaste; Burns notes that his friends' parents did not see him as a suitable friend for their children, given his whiteness and his family's poverty: 'The experience of being deemed undesirable and unworthy even by new Australians is a peculiarly lumpen trial. For me, it was eye-opening. For others, it's an unutterable humiliation.'[5]

Humiliation. It's a word I predominantly associate with the deep flush of shame I feel when I experience racism in my day-to-day life. As a teenager, I would never have considered that my tormentors could themselves have been acting out of a sense of unconscious humiliation. Sure, it's impossible for me to really know what their motives were at the time, but I only ever considered racism to be bred from ignorance, never that it might have come from a place of misguided fear. I associated whiteness with power, which is primarily the case – except that power is inherently hierarchical, and even white people can be poor and powerless, the last to receive the spoils of the capitalist societies that are built on their labour.

And when governments try to address issues like racism, especially in a country like Australia, which is built on power being taken away from Indigenous populations and given to white people, that hierarchy of power is applied to race, meaning that there's no real way of looking at the complexity of the issue without having to deconstruct all of that problematic distribution of power in the first place. It's much easier for the government to build programs on the idea of white people being the racists and brown people the victims, because delving into it too deeply is kind of at odds with the whole structure of our society.

But still, the Harmony Ambassador tour does seem like a particularly hollow attempt. How odd it seems now, to think that the government provided funds to send a bunch of ethnic teens to address an issue that has plagued mankind for centuries, armed with nothing but our kitsch traditional clothing and shallow attempts at disarming entertainment.

The irony of my being sent out into the world as an ambassador for cultural difference was lost on me at fourteen. Although I was still highly engaged with Indian culture, and was somewhat more openly proud of our traditions, I had already begun my quest to fit in with what I saw as Australian culture by separating myself from my Fijian-Indian heritage. So it could seem strange that I was part of a project that required me to passionately promote cultural difference. I suppose I felt that the private issues I was grappling with were separate from the broader societal issue of racism, which naturally I still unequivocally opposed. Plus, my dad – who always has my best interests at heart – wanted me to do it (and had in fact put my name forward when he saw a call-out for participants), *and* it was ten days out of school, so I had very few objections.

As it happened, the Harmony Ambassador tour did prove to be a cultural awakening for me, but in ways not linked to India or Fiji. Instead, I found myself discovering more about feminism, indie music and alternative fashion from one of our tutors. Jane was in her mid-twenties, and she was pretty much the coolest person I had ever met. She wore tie-dyed hippie clothes from Tree of Life, and had the kind of freckled, open face that screams earnestness. She worked part-time as an English tutor for migrant and refugee children, and was contracted to support us with our schoolwork for the duration of the tour.

Unlike most of the other young people on the tour, my English was good and I didn't require much guidance with school assignments. So when Jane and I sat together on the bus between towns, we talked about life, politics, art and eventually our personal goals and secrets. Jane gave me a CD she loved, *I'm Wide Awake, It's Morning* by Bright Eyes. The first strains of 'We Are Nowhere and It's Now' wove through my headphones, and I was stunned, completely caught in Conor

Oberst's crackling voice and the melancholy of the music. Weeks later, after the tour had ended, Jane gave me a card and a few small gifts, one of them a yellow bird pin that I still have today, a reference to the song.

With Jane, I talked about feminism, and the frustration I sometimes felt at the parts of Islam that made me feel that perhaps women weren't valued as highly throughout the wider Muslim community as in my immediate family. This was a difficult topic for me then; I was still quite a devout Muslim, but I was troubled by aspects of the religion. Jane listened without judgement, and allowed me to think out loud to her as I grappled with these questions. She encouraged me to write, and recommended books and music. Together we checked out the hippie stores that seem to be a fixture on high streets up and down the coast, and bought crystal necklaces and matching purple tie-dyed shirts.

I found in her both a friend and a portal into a future I still struggled to picture. Jane went to university, worked and lived in a share house. She told me about parties at her friends' houses, and kisses in corridors with men she liked. She dreamed of moving to Melbourne, a decision she could make for herself without anyone else's input or approval – a degree of freedom that I couldn't imagine. Crucially, Jane was the first adult on the tour who saw more in me than my Indian heritage. She recognised me as the weird mix of identities I really was (and still am), in the same way that my friends at school did, but the fact that she was older and didn't question my ability to be both Indian *and* into all the stuff I liked felt highly gratifying. Where peers like Melissa, my best friend at school, were my comrades in arms, Jane was more like a tour guide. Melissa and I bolstered each other's confidence on our shared journey of self-discovery, but Jane gave me a roadmap to becoming the person I wanted to be, lending me her confidence as armour for the journey.

I was immersed in a program that focused on a singular feature of my identity – the differences that made me a target for prejudice and linked me to an 'othered' community. But with Jane, I discovered parts of myself – the songs that made my heart skip, the possibilities that filled me with yearning – that would ultimately create a barrier between me and the Fijian-Indian heritage I was working to normalise at high school assemblies and council dinners. At the heart of this dissonance was the ultimate flaw of the Harmony Ambassador program: by showcasing aspects of our cultures like fleeting entertainment on a variety show, the program implicitly reinforced the notion that POC are inherently different from white people, essentialising us into our specific races.

Each of us stood in as a symbol of our race, which meant that we were carrying the invisible burden of a stereotype – because it's impossible for any individual to do justice to an entire culture in a meaningful way. I imagine that my fellow ambassadors felt a personal connection to the dances they performed and the poetry they recited, but I know for a fact that they cared about so much more than that. The Pacific

Islands girls loved doing their traditional dance, but they also *loved* getting down to a Destiny's Child song back in our hotel rooms; the Russian boy wrote eloquent poetry about his home, but he could also talk your ear off about Aussie Rules football. We were, and still are, more than any one cultural label can contain, but the Harmony Ambassador tour might as well have replaced our names with the names of our countries and left it at that.

By the same logic that informed the program, we as ambassadors should have felt connected to each other on the basis of our cultural heritage above all else. So I should have felt closest to Rita, the other Indian girl on the tour, but instead I found myself drifting on the outskirts of the group, spending the most time with Jane. Rita was so enthusiastic about Indian culture that I sometimes felt as though I was being tested when she asked me what I thought of a recent Bollywood film, or whether my mother cooked certain dishes at home. Nothing other than our skin colour connected Rita and me. It was a feeling I recognised from trying to befriend the other Indian girls at school, only to realise that we had nothing in common. Being Indian was just what I was made of – but who I *actually was* was based on so much more.

Perhaps it wasn't the tour's intention to create these cultural cages, and I hope that the audiences realised that people are multifaceted and can be into and influenced by many different things at the same time. But I didn't see how the tour could hope to dismantle racist attitudes by focusing on shallow cultural tropes. I couldn't help but think it might have been more effective to conduct small group discussions with the students, giving them the chance to actually talk to us. Yet the ethnic extravaganza rolled on, and we continued to travel like gypsies from one small town to the next, broadcasting our message of harmony – except we had no idea if anyone was really listening.

It's now more than a decade since the Harmony Ambassador tour (to my knowledge it never ran again), and if anything, the country seems to be drifting further from racial harmony. The re-election of Pauline Hanson to the Senate in 2016 felt like a massive leap backwards, an indicator that things have become drastically worse.

Regardless of how many times a new 'Humans of [insert suburb here]' webpage shares a migrant narrative, or the number of #I'llRideWithYou campaigns the well-intentioned left releases, cultural diversity remains the realm of the marginalised and villainised. This lack of progress is partly due to the economic and social issues Shannon Burns describes, but is also a result of the continued attempts to normalise cultural difference without acknowledging its complexity.

If we are to meaningfully engage with the concept of racial equality, it will mean dismantling the benevolent categorising of POC according to stereotypes of their culture that both the government and the progressive left have thus far based their multicultural messaging on. And it will mean no longer relying on randomly assigned 'community leaders' to represent a particular culture, giving one person the opportunity to speak on behalf of their race and avoiding other views in case they contradict the messaging that has been approved.

British-Indian author Kenan Malik has labelled the latter practice 'community gatekeeping'. In his article 'Away With the Gatekeepers', Malik interrogates the validity of assigning one person the power to speak on behalf of a community. He points to examples in Europe where the 'so-called community leaders' are 'frequently religious, often conservative, and rarely representative of their communities'.[6] As he notes, these 'community leaders' are often self-appointed and may use their power more to shut down debate *within* their community than to shelter the community from external attacks. Differences of opinion naturally arise within any community, but it is in the interests of these community leaders to promote a homogenous view of their culture that is aligned with their own identity, as the group with the loudest voice stands to gain the largest spoils.

Growing up, I saw this false leadership in action. I knew, for example, that a small group of men led our local Muslim community in Canberra, and I heard about the conflicts that arose within this group. Part of the issue was that Islam is diverse and varies widely across different cultural groups: how could any small committee truly represent the wide range of practices and beliefs within our local Muslim community in multicultural Canberra?

As Malik says, unofficial community leaders – the people who end up running the local cultural society, or coordinating their country's display at the International Festival each year – are seldom democratically elected. They are selected by virtue of their own drive and motivation, but there is no mechanism for the general population of their culture to have a say in this. All it means is that only the loudest voices are heard and everyone else has to accept it. Sometimes this is fine – in fact, I am grateful for the initiative and commitment of the men and women who coordinate our Eid celebrations each year, or who put together the local Islamic women's network. But when this unofficial leadership is relied on to inform government policies that affect the wider group, it becomes more complicated. Without a multitude of voices, we are always going to leave people behind.

In the case of the Harmony Ambassador tour, from what I can tell, each of the participants was selected on the recommendation of 'community leaders' who decided that we were appropriate young people to showcase our cultures. We were community leaders in training.

The role feels so false to me now – I was in no position to represent the young Indian migrant population, whom I barely interacted with beyond my siblings. Having my personal experience amplified to include the experiences of everyone else who looked like me was a huge responsibility, and certainly not one I could effectively take on as a teenager. Might the project have been more effective if, rather than bringing in a handful of young people from Canberra, the organisers had supported the creation of dialogues between people from different faiths, cultural backgrounds and interests within the communities we visited, to build a sense of ambassadorship from within each community?

Of course, community leaders can act with the best possible intentions and still contribute to the exclusion of members of their communities who are already on the fringe. Look at someone like Yassmin Abdel-Magied, a talented and passionate young woman who is proud of her Muslim faith and is regularly called on by the media to speak on any issue relating to Australian Muslims. I get the impression that regardless of what Yassmin is interested in or has demonstrated experience of, the media expects her to be able to speak for all Muslims, on any topic under the sun. Yassmin and I both grew up in Australia, raised as Muslims, at a similar point in time. Yet we are at opposite ends of the religious spectrum. Yassmin is deeply connected to her faith, and highly engaged in the Muslim community. I am an apostate, an atheist, on the outskirts of the cultural community I once belonged to. Where Yassmin has proclaimed on national television that Islam is a 'feminist religion',[7] I am not a Muslim precisely because Islam, to me, is *not* a feminist religion.

I have always struggled with the position of women in the Quran as secondary to men. Of course, like all religious texts, the Quran is open to interpretation – which is why only allowing a few voices to be heard on the topic of religion is so problematic. When I speak about these issues online, I usually encounter silence from the Australians who claim to care about multiculturalism and supporting minority voices. My experience of Islam as both a positive and negative force in my life contradicts the progressive anti-Islamophobia rhetoric, which seems to promote an all-encompassing view of Islam as inherently peaceful and feminist, save for the minority of Muslims who are classified as 'extremists'. This attitude comes from a desire to end prejudice against Muslims, but it has the negative side effect of silencing people like me, who still bear the brunt of prejudice against Muslims by virtue of our race but are not supported within the Muslim community because we no longer practise the religion we were raised with.

The mainstream left can't conceive of both Yassmin and me existing and having equally valid experiences, because the pro-multiculturalism rhetoric is about homogenising cultures, not embracing their multitudes. It's as if my contradicting Yassmin, while still being a left-wing progressive-minded individual, and still deeply respecting Islam and enjoying the aspects of the religion that I can engage in with my family, will cause some sort of spontaneous combustion in the well-meaning white person who just wants to show support to one Muslim and have that imply generalised support to every Muslim, without getting too deep into what every Muslim might be like as an individual.

Of course Australian multiculturalism is tokenistic, if this is the basis of our attempts to be inclusive of all cultures. The

Harmony Ambassador tour was really the logical continuation of government policy, which otherwise promotes multiculturalism through annual 'festivals' where people converge to eat food and watch entertainment from different cultures. But meaningful multiculturalism would be so much more than that – it would ultimately mean letting go of the concept of racial identity preceding other personal traits, and confronting the violent colonial history of this country.

It would mean seeing a person such as myself as a feminist, a writer, an animal rights activist, an environmentalist and a lover of baked goods who just happens to also be Indian. It would mean valuing the apostates, the 'Oreos' and 'coconuts', the dissidents, the not-easily-characterised, as much as the faithful, the culturally proud, the new-to-English and 'fresh off the boat' individuals who unintentionally fulfil the assumptions and stereotypes that currently pervade our media landscape.

It would mean genuinely attempting to focus on a shared Australian identity that is less about lamingtons and surf lifesavers, and more about honouring and acknowledging the Indigenous cultures that have inhabited this land for millennia, and the transient, ever-changing nature of contemporary Australia.

It would mean allowing Yassmin and me to share a stage and talk about our conflicting experiences, and rather than seeing this as demonstrating flaws in the foundations of Australian Muslim culture, instead focusing on the amazing way in which Australia can support diversity *within* cultures, not just between them.

Malik, in writing on the flaws of an identity-based approach to racism and multiculturalism, points out that 'at the heart of multiculturalism is a confusion of political equality and cultural identity. Equality of cultural identity is not the same as political equality. Indeed, it undermines the possibility of any such equality.'[8] Just because many Australians living in regional towns, on lower incomes and with fewer social and economic opportunities are white doesn't undo the fact that they are suffering from political inequality. Similarly, while I suffer some discrimination and prejudice based on my race, and while I carry the colonial burden of the oppression of my ancestors with me to a degree, I also benefit from the capitalist system that keeps the poor white working class down so that it can lift me – a beneficiary of social mobility – up. Until we look at these social and structural roots of racism as they intersect with political and economic inequality, POC will continue to be the unwilling scapegoats for the frustrations of the white working class, and vice versa.

More than a decade on, it's hard for me to see what the Harmony Ambassador tour achieved for cultural harmony in Australia's regional communities. I wonder if anyone remembers our performances, and whether the students talked about the issues further after we left. I wonder if I'll ever see Jane again, so I can thank her for her support and her ability to see me as more than just my skin colour.

The tour was filmed and eventually made into a DVD. I have a copy but I've never watched it, unsure whether I really want to relive that time, and whether my far more critical adult's perspective would tear apart the positive experiences I had while on the tour.

A few months ago, while packing for a temporary move to Scotland, I put almost all of my DVDs into a box for donation. But that one I kept, staring at the dull brown cover. I held it, and the photo album from the tour, and the journal I wrote in every day. I haven't opened any of them in years, but I couldn't bring myself to throw them away. Instead, I packed them into the bottom of a storage box, and covered them with my Joy Division CDs, novels and DVD box sets of *Gilmore Girls*. The action was a metaphor for my selfhood that was a tad too obvious, much like the tour itself.

KINDRED SPIRITS

I can think of my life in two distinct chapters. In the first chapter I was a solitary creature, my company books, pets and worlds made entirely from my own imagination. The second chapter of my life was when friendship finally seemed a possibility.

I didn't have the best introduction to schoolyard friendship. Growing up in Albury in the early 1990s as one of the few non-white kids at my school (the others being my siblings), I learned to fear other kids, and to feel subconsciously ashamed of my skin colour. During the years we attended primary school in Albury, I endured slurs about being dirty, and my sisters and I were followed home from the bus stop by boys who told us we were 'brown like poo'. I also had to contend with ongoing ostracism that meant that from one day to the next I either had a friend or didn't, depending on the whims of the white girls who didn't want my difference to taint them. Zaheeda would come across from the senior school (she was in year six at the time) to visit me at recess. As well as dosing me with Ventolin for my asthma, she would (firmly) encourage some of the girls in my class to play with me. The seven-year-olds in question rolled their eyes but grudgingly agreed – my big sister is very persuasive – and I tottered along behind them, desperate to make friends but somehow unable to make it stick.

I had friends (eventually, and after a lot of heartache) but no kindred spirits of the Anne Shirley/Diana Barry variety. Through it all, I felt a sense of yearning. I knew there must be people who were fascinated by the same things that enthralled me – novels, music, imagined futures. But they weren't near me, and I had no clue where to find them.

Things began to change when we moved to Canberra. My new primary school was very multicultural – so much so that I was initially a little bemused that I didn't stand out anymore, having got used to bracing myself for unwanted attention. This swiftly turned to relief, but things didn't immediately fall into place. Although there was no more bullying, I still didn't entirely fit in. The years of schoolyard taunts and self-hatred had made me unwilling to put myself out there, preferring small groups to the unpredictability of larger ones. I was also a bit socially inept, far more comfortable hiding behind a book than making conversation. Where my charismatic siblings made friends easily, played sport and generally went with the flow, I couldn't catch a ball or run very far, tried to keep riding a tricycle after the age of five, and couldn't make a friend to save my life.

As a child obsessed with *Anne of Green Gables*, I hoped to meet a true kindred spirit, but no such person came along. I had some close friends at my new primary school in Canberra, and they were all excellent people, but at some point we would always drift apart. Looking back, I'm not sure whether this was a result of the natural changes that happen when you transition from primary to high school, or whether I was just particularly bad at making friendships last. In any case, I wasn't exactly hot property in the friendship market.

I also suffered from the less obvious demerits of cultural difference. I wasn't allowed to go to sleepovers past the age of twelve, my parents preferring that my friends came to our house so we would be under their supervision. This made for lots of fun parties at my place, but it also meant missing out on those held at my friends' houses. On mufti days, when other girls came to school in the cutest miniskirts, I would be wearing a *salwar kameez*, or something else demure and modest – the unofficial uniform of a Good Muslim Girl. School holidays were taken up with family activities, either travelling to Fiji or New Zealand to visit relatives, or packed with plans for just the six of us – all great fun, but still drastically cutting into time I could have spent with friends. I felt too ashamed to practise any Spice Girls dances at recess when I knew Allah was watching, and I couldn't even eat the food everyone else liked. One year I went to a birthday party with hot dogs on the menu and was given a banana in a bun by a bewildered white mother trying to figure out what *halal* meant.

But neither could I bring myself to join the crowd of South Asian girls in my school who hung out together. These girls were as proud of their cultural heritage as they were of their hip-hop dancing and adoration of *The O.C.* Even in Indian circles I was weird. I loved reading fantasy books, and was obsessed with Harry Potter and the band The Whitlams, in a way that seemed a bit too . . . white. Without access to the internet until much later in adolescence, and with limited access to culture outside of Indian movies and music, I always felt a few steps behind everyone else, Indian or not.

Don't get me wrong, I had fun. My best friends were my mother and sisters, and our family was close in a way that always felt special. As part of our culture, our relationships with each other and our extended relatives were particularly close, amplified by the time we spent together after school and on weekends. The bond between my siblings, my parents and me runs deep. Family dinners were full of jokes and laughter, and my sisters and I could spend hours talking without getting sick of each other (in between the usual sibling fights, of course). But there were some things I just knew they wouldn't get. Like the stories I spent hours scribbling into notebooks, or my obsession with the few alternative fashion stores in town. As I got older, I wanted to share these interests with other people, but neither my family nor my few friends were curious about the things that lit me up with excitement.

That all changed in my first year at high school. A primary school friend, Alexis, pointed out to me a girl she had met. 'That's Melissa,' she said. 'She likes horses!' This was a favour to me (and to herself too). I was horse mad, and Alexis was distinctly not. Horse crazy or not, this Melissa girl, who was short and wiry, with beautiful silky blonde hair in a long ponytail down her back, seemed alright to me. I didn't know it then, but I had met a true kindred spirit.

In our fifteen years of friendship, Melissa and I have graduated from one obsession to another, always in synchronicity. From horses and Harry Potter we moved on to *Gilmore Girls*, zines, writing, literature, indie rock music, manga, poetry slams, house parties, cats, coffee, vegetarianism, animal welfare, art galleries, backpacking through Europe and, most recently, dog memes . . . She remains the person I message with the latest cool thing or bemusing question, knowing she will always *get it*. Most importantly, she's the person who, in some ways, introduced me to myself.

We exchanged mix CDs, and talked endlessly about the books we devoured. We both had accounts on FictionPress.com, where we published our own short stories (and long stories), and read addictive amateur romance plots. We passed scissors, glue sticks and a bowl of M&Ms between us as we cut and pasted together our mini-magazine of poetry, fiction and observations that we would eventually leave out for strangers to pick up at Impact Comics in Canberra city, with not even a hint of embarrassment at our own audacity.

Gradually, too, we pushed each other to go to public events, to write for different outlets, to go to gigs and meet new people. Both of us were naturally a little shy, but we were able to explore these new environments secure in the knowledge that we had each other's back. It was a cultural awakening, and an introduction to a creative world I had only ever glimpsed before. I began to stretch my own creative muscles, each new experience pulling taut the cord that tied me to my family and to the limits of Indian expectations. I never showed our zines to my parents, because I knew they wouldn't necessarily understand the appeal of cut and pasting pages together and then broadcasting our amateur scribblings to the public. I *definitely* didn't share my fanfiction or confessional teenage writing with my family, full as it was of romance and adolescent angst, which I knew they wouldn't approve of my sharing with strangers on the internet.

In this, and despite our closeness, the real difference between Melissa and me was revealed. Where Melissa could travel freely, my every step was closely counted, and the result of a hundred small bargains and deceptions that allowed me to nudge the boundary of what was acceptable for a Good Indian Girl to experience.

Melissa and I were sitting in the back row of our year nine Indonesian class. We were the only two from our friendship group who took Indonesian, which meant that for four years we had four hours a week of uninterrupted hanging-out time. Uninterrupted partly because we never shut up, and partly because our Indonesian teacher had a pleasantly lax attitude to classroom behaviour. As otherwise diligent students, Melissa and I started each year intending to try to do well in Indonesian, but inevitably gave up and spent our lessons talking about books, magazines and TV shows we loved.

Every year nine student at our school had to complete a week of work experience. I was unsure where to apply – I wanted to be a writer, but as far as I could tell the only way to make money from writing was by working for a major daily. I couldn't think of anything worse than spending a week at *The Canberra Times*, which I saw as boring and stuffy (and also extremely intimidating).

'I'm going to email this magazine I like – it's even produced in Canberra,' Melissa told me. She held out a copy of a glossy mag with a bright yellow-and-black-striped cover. The title – a pink logo in the corner – was *Lip*.

Flipping through the magazine, I was intrigued. There were articles by gay teenagers about coming out to their parents, and a quiz helping the reader identify what kind of feminist they were. There were punk rock fashion spreads, and girls of all shapes and sizes grinning at the camera. I don't think I'd ever seen anything that cool. Even then, Melissa had a unique talent for sniffing out cultural artefacts that were quirky and ahead of their time. She had an understated way of consuming music, film and books that was always about genuine enjoyment and never about showing off to her peers. This was at a time in our lives when every little thing about us was dissected within the social sphere of high school, and if you wanted to be popular it was crucial to like the 'right' things. Our friendship group was distinctly behind in those stakes, and we had basically embraced that and stopped trying to fit in with the popular kids at school a while ago. When you get pegged with fruit at lunchtime for no obvious reason, and your peers describe you as 'weird' and 'freaks', you tend to grow a thick skin. Doing work experience at *Lip* might sound cool now, but back then it was just more ammunition to prove that we were losers. In 2004, there was nothing more lame than feminism.

'Would you hate me if I stole your idea?' I said, still gazing at the magazine in my hands.

'Of course not. It'll be cool to do it together,' said Melissa. Another teenager might have held their cultural discoveries close to their chest, but not her.

So both of us did 'internships' with *Lip* for our work experience, and then volunteered at an all-day arts festival it hosted. Afterwards, I started writing for the magazine. In 2005 it published my first ever article, and I eventually started contributing a monthly column. Melissa stayed involved too, but *Lip* swiftly turned into 'my' thing, as I became more and more involved with the publication.

At the time, I had no idea what a seminal moment it was when Melissa handed me the magazine. I didn't know that I would go on to edit *Lip*, or that this would develop my skills as a writer and editor, eventually leading to the launch of my own feminist website, Feminartsy. Under an unspoken agreement, both Melissa and I pursued our writing careers and never competed with each other. Melissa became a widely published film critic and the editor of the film section of the local street mag, and I continued working with *Lip*, our paths parallel but never crossing over in a way that could lead to issues in our friendship.

I doubt Melissa had any idea what she was helping to kickstart for me either, but I often look back on the unselfish way in which she shared her discovery with me. If the roles had been reversed and I had found *Lip* first, I can't say for sure that I would have shared it with Melissa until I had already established my own relationship with the magazine. Melissa wasn't so single-minded, and she is still generous in that way now.

Even then, she had a clear understanding of the limits I faced within my culture. She knew implicitly not to mention *Lip* around my parents until I had shared it with them, knowing they might be anxious about me writing publicly at such a young age about things like gender, culture and identity. When I occasionally called her in tears over not being allowed to attend an event or sleepover, she knew that I needed an ear and a shoulder, but no criticism of my family. (I'm the only one allowed to criticise them!) She was there when I started unravelling my religious identity; seeing past our differences to the ways that we were similar, she offered me advice based on that shared understanding of life. In the most harrowing moments of my life, Melissa was a constant support.

October 2009 in Newcastle was unbelievably rainy, but the bad weather couldn't dampen our enthusiasm as we rolled into town for the This Is Not Art Festival. It felt like an important rite of passage – for the past two years Melissa and I had watched the festival online, pondering how to get there, given that while we were in high school, my parents didn't want me going on trips with friends without adult supervision. But now we were eighteen, and Mum and Dad had agreed that I could make the trip to Newcastle for what I described as a writers' festival (without noting how left-of-centre and quirky it is).

On our first night in Newcastle, we went to The Crack House for a performance by Mr Fibby, a musical group from Canberra whom we adored. They performed to raucous appreciation, and we felt maybe unjustifiably proud that we shared a hometown.

For the rest of the weekend, we lurked in the back of crowded rooms to watch panel events, or wandered through crazy theatre performances in abandoned buildings, a little nervous of each new experience but glad to be there together. When a group of elegant Melbourne hipsters walked by, we glanced at each other, tacitly sharing an appreciation of their style, and a desire to be a little more like these effortlessly alternative people.

We shared a room in a holiday rental apartment and fingered through our haul of zines in the evening, gathering inspiration for our next attempt at publishing. It was thrilling to be immersed in the independent publishing scene, to hear from writers we admired, and to glimpse what our own careers could look like. It was something I hadn't dared to dream I would experience – I was so sure that my parents would never allow me to come.

It said a lot about Melissa that my parents trusted us to travel together. She was the only friend whose house I could stay at overnight without my mother worrying. I was gently testing the boundaries with my parents, first going to gigs at the university, then staying overnight at Melissa's, and now this trip away, each new step another chance to prove that nothing bad would happen to me if I spent a night away from them.

Melissa is one of the few friends who always took my cultural restrictions into consideration when planning our outings. She would offer her couch for me to sleep on, or agree to go to things earlier so we could leave in time for me to make it home before curfew. She never made a fuss about these compromises, willing to take the hit to her own social capital if it meant I could come too. I sometimes felt embarrassed when my brother had to join us at a show, or we had to make sure we left a gig by 11 pm, but Melissa always shrugged it off. It was more fun when we were together, she assured me.

On mornings after a gig night or party, I could see the truth in her words – sleep deprivation is better shared, as are trips to the Dickson shops in Canberra for a greasy breakfast. I would drive us to the cafe in my beaten-up car, and we talked the whole time – about life, university, our future plans. I lived for these conversations, in which we tried to figure ourselves out. It was a mutual enterprise, because we each needed the other's perspective to help us uncover our own identities.

But sometimes I felt as though I was only play-acting during these 'deep and meaningfuls'. I joined in the discussion about moving into a share house together, but I never really believed it would happen. My parents wouldn't allow me to live out of home while still being in the same city as them, at least not without a lot of to and fro. In our culture, the best way to secure your children's safety and modesty is to keep them at home until they are married. My sisters moved away for university, but that was sanctioned only because they were in university housing and there was some level of supervision. Moving out in Canberra when I could have kept living at home was symbolic of much more than just a change of address – it was a signal to our community that I wasn't behaving as a Good Indian Daughter is expected to.

It wasn't that my parents didn't trust me; rather, they didn't trust the world, and were too aware of all the things that could go wrong. I knew that when I got home at midnight and my father was still up, reading a book, it was because he couldn't rest until he knew where his children were. I knew that if I moved out my mother would lie awake at night wondering whether I had driven home safely, whether I had enough to eat or enough money for rent. I also knew how lucky I was to have parents who provided for me so generously, who would never let me want for anything, and who only demanded my honesty and adherence to their values in return. I knew that their protectiveness was as much about love as it was about tradition and honour.

But I still wanted to be out on my own – I just had no idea how to get there.

Increasingly I see the idea of individual freedom as a white concept. We can only make certain choices for ourselves if we have the resources to do so – if we have money, and a place to sleep, and an education to build those choices around. For my parents growing up in Fiji – where opportunities were few, income was unpredictable and government assistance difficult to access – community was considered far more important than individual freedom. Family and selflessness are at the heart of the culture that I was raised within – a culture that is a medley of Fijian-Indian and Muslim, and my parents' distinct personalities. Self-determination is a conceit, and the wellbeing of the majority is prioritised. There's a reason why there aren't many nursing homes in India and Fiji – it's because parents live the last years of their lives in their children's home, a practice that is accepted by the children not just as a duty but as a privilege. Looking after our elderly parents is repayment for the sacrifices they have made to give us the best possible life.

This kind of family bond is maintained through rituals. For example, if a man has sisters, when the son or daughter of their sister gets married, he will give that sister money or a gift, and when a woman is married, her sisters ceremonially welcome the groom to the wedding to show that he is now their brother, their relationship like one of blood. The ceremony indicates that from that day on, he is someone they can rely on, and he can equally rely on them – blood is blood, whether by birth or marriage.

When put like this, the cultural emphasis on family over all other relationships seems difficult to critique. As I grow older myself and watch my nieces and nephew grow up, I feel an echo of the fierce protectiveness I have no doubt my parents felt with my siblings and me. Who other than their family, both immediate and extended, will ensure their safety, that they are loved and given every chance to succeed? Who makes the sacrifices that mean they can be free to learn and grow, even if it means that they grow apart and away from us?

I have always felt guilty that I am unable to align my personal desires with what my parents wanted for me. I wish I could have been personally committed to their religion, and that I could have wanted and found a husband who was suitable in their eyes. I wish I didn't want to be so independent, and that my goals and aspirations hadn't required a slow unpicking of the identity I was raised with.

It took me three years to move out. At eighteen I started to plan, focusing on dreams of what my future could be in order to quell the panic that rose in my throat whenever I thought about telling my parents. Part of the guilt I felt at moving out was because I had a particularly good lifestyle at home, with everything I could possibly need. My parents were generous with all four of their children – we had every comfort, from the food we ate to the beds we slept in. It was a privileged life. The knowledge of that privilege sometimes made me feel physically ill. I felt ungrateful and afraid of the hurt I would cause my parents. But deep down I also knew that this feeling was not justified – that moving out did not have to be a rejection of everything I was given. That it could just be a necessary step towards becoming my own person.

But it was also a massive step for my family, and hugely different from the path followed by most children of Muslim Fijian-Indian migrants. No one in our broader family or community networks had ever moved out of home before marriage except to go to university, with the understanding they would move back home unless married at the end of their studies. I knew that to my aunts and uncles, and to the wider community, my choice to live out of home permanently as an unmarried woman would suggest something unacceptable about me – that I was stepping away from our culture, that I was becoming more white than I was Indian. This fear was born of a racial stereotyping of white people (not dissimilar to that which we faced as Indians in Australia) as being somehow immoral in comparison to us – a stereotype which is no doubt harmful, yet which is widely accepted as fact in the communities I grew up in. How would my family know where I slept at night, that my virtue was intact? How could potential husbands be sure of this? It would be hard for my parents to explain to others; but more than that, it would mean they were failing to provide the protection that they felt bound to give to me, and relinquishing their ability to keep me safe. A lot of their negative stance on my moving out came from cultural attitudes, but there was also a strong sentiment of sadness at having a child fly the nest, especially their youngest, whom they weren't ready to let go of yet. It was an incredibly complex time, and I have no idea how tumultuous and difficult it must have been for my parents, on their side of the debate.

Moving out became a huge source of tension, and we had numerous arguments and discussions. I know that my mother dreaded me raising the topic, but I couldn't let it go – I knew deep in my bones that I had to live away from home before I could ever agree to marriage, because I desperately wanted to get to know myself outside of my family, as an adult. It had to happen, and my parents knew it had to happen eventually too, which is why they finally gave in.

'I'd rather have you move out with our blessing than risk losing you forever by fighting,' Mum said to me, a stance that

I still reflect on as being full of grace, considering how she felt about my decision.

Through all of this – the arguments, the tears – Melissa was my comforter and supporter. She was the one who would send me concerned text messages, to make sure I was okay and not too upset. She was the one who quietly arranged for a different housemate to take the room that was going to be mine, when she realised I couldn't make the leap that year. She was the one who wrote about my strength and courage in my birthday card each year, and offered her solidarity.

I leaned on Melissa, because her life often felt like a projection of the one I was seeking – our paths ran on almost parallel tracks, but mine had bumps and detours where hers struck out in a mostly straight, solid line. She had moved out at eighteen, and it seemed effortless to me. I remember her parents driving her things to her house, and meeting her every weekend for brunch and a family walk. My memories of that first year of university revolve around hanging out at her place, while she poured M&Ms into a tub of ice cream for dinner.

As with everything Melissa did, her new life looked breezy and fun. I don't doubt that she worked hard for it, but the work she did – the jobs, the studying, balancing her finances – was for the most part a different kind of hard from the work I did. My work was emotional, entrenched, generational. It involved interrogating a culture that was born out of colonialism and strife and fear of change, because change was seldom a choice in Fiji and India. I had to undertake this work while also carrying the emotional baggage of my parents, and the generations before them. My very existence in Australia was a product of multiple journeys – from India to Fiji, by choice and by coercion, through poverty and violence and displacement – finishing with the one that eventually put three-year-old me onto a plane.

Finally, at the age of 21, that journey led me to a dodgy Dickson share house, staring at the ceiling and trying to ignore the shrieking of possums that emanated through its cracks while I scratched at the inflamed bites on my legs. A few weeks after I had moved in with Melissa and one other girl, our share house became infested with fleas. It's still disputed where they came from, but over the next few days the situation reached peak absurdity. We stomped around the house in 32-degree heat wearing nightdresses and gumboots. Every time a foot landed on carpet, dozens of tiny black missiles would jump onto our calves. My legs were so covered in bites they looked like one shiny red mass, and they hurt like hell. Friends stopped coming around, and we battled with the real-estate agent to figure out who should pay for the fleas' eradication.

One morning, after an uncomfortable night spent scratching my various bites, I blearily lifted the doona and looked under it to see fleas jumping relentlessly onto my flesh. It took all of my strength not to scream. Instead, I stuffed my sheets and doona into garbage bags, and then the garbage bags into more garbage bags, and dragged the whole sorry mess to my car.

I drove to my parents' house (a good thirty minutes away), as if fleeing an actual plague.

I moved out, and I immediately got fleas, I kept thinking, shaking my head at the sheer insanity of the situation. I used my keys to get into the house, stomped straight to the laundry and put my linen into a high-speed wash. 'Drown, you arseholes,' I muttered.

I trudged away into the lounge room, surprising my mother, who was watching the morning news. She was so delighted to see me, I could have cried. Sitting there an hour later, eating the fresh scones Mum whipped up, on a clean couch with no fleas in sight, I felt both grateful and a little disappointed in my own lack of resilience. Being there felt like admitting defeat. I couldn't survive without my family. I couldn't even live free of vermin without my family.

Mum's delighted welcome was the fruit of years of her emotional labour. By the time I actually moved out, she was determined to be supportive, even though it was difficult for her to understand my choices. By waiting – and pushing through our opposing perspectives on what moving out signified – I could now come home and enjoy my mother's nurturing without feeling the stress I had felt before. But I still wanted to prove to them that I *could* live successfully out of home, that I was as independent in practice as I had always claimed to be. The fleas were a failure, I felt, and confirmed Mum's (unspoken but obvious) opinion that our crumbling share house was a bit of a tip.

When I returned to my new home, it was to find Melissa and our other housemate placing flea bombs throughout the house. After setting them off we congregated on the porch, exchanging relieved and oddly exuberant glances. We were doing it, and we were doing it alone. Melissa had been taking care of this kind of stuff for two years, and was now able to get on with it without running to her mother. My resilience was only just beginning to grow, and had required a home-cooked meal to even emerge in the first place. I felt ashamed of my weakness, but also relieved that I was with my more experienced friends.

The fear and frustration I felt around moving out, I eventually realised, was similar to my reaction to sleepovers as a child. My parents still joke about how they would come home from dropping me off and then wait by the phone for the inevitable call a few hours later, asking them to pick me up. I remember going to these sleepovers and having fun for about an hour, and then noticing my friend's parents having a moment of affection, maybe an embrace and kiss on the lips. This was alien to me – my parents love each other, but the propriety demanded in our culture and religion mean they would never demonstrate affection in this way. I would feel a sort of dread swoop over me, and my six-year-old brain would panic. These people were not Indians, and they weren't Muslim, and they had no clue how I lived. They didn't know I had to eat *halal* food. They didn't get that my feet couldn't face in the direction of Mecca when I slept, because that would be an insult to Allah. They didn't understand that I needed to brush my teeth *before* breakfast, to rid the staleness of the night from my mouth. Looking back, I assume that my parents would have spoken to my friends' parents about these things, but as a child I was simply overwhelmed by our differences. I would stare at my own hands and notice, as if for the first time, how incredibly brown I was. I would look at the people around me and realise just how strange they were to me.

This same feeling of alienation haunted my first few weeks of living out of home as an adult, when I realised that no one was waiting for me at night, and no one would necessarily be awake and watching the morning news when I got up each day. The only thing that helped me settle in this strange new environment was having Melissa there.

In the years following our first share house – years that saw us move to different cities, and embark on our careers; years that saw both of us enter into long-term relationships, and coach each other through various challenges, heartbreaks, moves, failures and successes; years that saw us drift apart and then flow back together, skyping from overseas or sending cards in the mail; years that never passed without some contact, and some reminder that we are here for each other – Melissa and I have both continued to move forward on mostly parallel paths. Our cultural difference continues to be the only point at which we diverge.

Only in the past few years have I realised that comparing my own experiences to any white Australian's, as if they are starting from the exact same ground, is unfair. In most obvious ways, Melissa and I are more alike than we are different. We grew up in the same town, went to mostly the same schools, both have postgraduate qualifications, both work in communications and do freelance writing, love the same music and watch the same TV shows, and both read voraciously and travel overseas whenever we can. But where Melissa has been able to accept each new experience as something she has earned for herself, mine are part of a shared attainment as a result of immigration. My ability to study, to work, to earn money and then spend that money on the things I enjoy is a direct result of my parents studying immeasurably harder, working in less favourable conditions and for far less money, so that we could eventually migrate to Australia. Even then, the money they earned was saved and valued, and our pleasurable experiences were delivered for far less than I would now spend without a second thought. All of that work and sweat and fear and unbelonging, just so I could eventually rent an apartment in Canberra and watch Netflix on my laptop each night. Undoubtedly, Melissa's parents also worked hard to provide opportunities for their children, but that work didn't automatically require them to relinquish parts of their identity that were important to them, like their country of birth, their mother tongue and their extended family. That was a cost that my parents had to bear in order to obtain the security and opportunities of a first-world country for their children.

Crucially, in that legacy lies the foundation for the guilt that sticks to everything I do. Guilt for my parents' sacrifices, for my own privilege, for my distance and difference from women my age who still live in Fiji or India and aren't part of the small ruling elite and can't access the things I take for granted. Guilt for the western perspective that means I automatically assume that all women in those countries are inherently worse off than I am when I don't have any evidence to suggest this. Guilt for my future children, who will be another step removed from their heritage, who will feel even more unbelonging than I do. And guilt springing from the fundamental truth that I would never give up my current life, would never willingly go back to the countries that made me, because the privilege I have now is too valuable to give back.

When I spend time with Melissa now, I feel more at peace with our differences than I used to. When I was younger, I wanted so badly for us to be as similar as possible that I almost resented Melissa for her whiteness, and I hated myself for my brownness. This unconscious negativity influenced our relationship in subtle ways. I know there were times when she felt awkward in her own happiness and freedom – travelling overseas with friends or going out on the town – because I couldn't have those same things. I was often moody at these times, unable to separate Melissa the person from my jealousy over the difference in our circumstances. Now, I simply relish our friendship, and the ways in which our differences have enabled us to be better friends to each other. We are kindred spirits in part because of our similarities, but also because our similarities exist despite our differences. The fact that we found each other and forged a deep friendship in spite of the barriers created by cultural difference is a testament to our connection.

Most importantly, I feel an overwhelming gratitude to Melissa, and for the numerous other kindred spirits I have since met – almost exclusively women who have lifted me up, or allowed me to lift them up, and who have loved me unconditionally in a way that is special and beautiful. The fact of who I am is so often reduced to essentialised notions of race, or gender, or purpose. My friends, however, have always seen past those stereotypes to my true identity. It is in those friendships that I have been introduced to aspects of myself I'd had no idea existed.

That Melissa unreservedly believed, without ever consciously considering it, that I could love art and feminism and literature just as much as she did was a more radical act than I think either of us knew. Together, we bridged a divide that had been constructed from centuries of racial prejudice that assumed our skin colour made us so fundamentally different that our friendship would taint both of us.

Instead, we have shown that there is a universality to human interests, one that can make a brown girl and a white girl equally swoony when they hear the opening notes of a Bright

Eyes song, and equally furious when they read *A Room of One's Own*. And we have shown that a friendship, even one with as many mountains and valleys as ours has traversed, can hold tight through difference, in defiance of all that would keep us apart.

WHEN 'CHAI' IS 'TEA', AND 'CHAI TEA' IS 'TEA TEA'

I have been complimented on a range of things in my life, some of which are worth being proud of, and others not so much. My speedy typing (especially as I primarily use two fingers) is a skill I am always keen for people to notice; my ability to bend my fingers back on both hands thanks to double-jointed fingers to the point that I can catch a ball with the back of my hand is pretty cool; and I don't mind being showered with praise for my baking. But the thing I get complimented on too often for it to be comfortable is my grasp of the English language.

At least once every two months or so some well-meaning stranger will tell me how good my English is, usually with a patronising smile. I imagine the thought process is that I am brown, therefore I will speak broken English with a strong accent, and when I don't they are surprised to the point of commenting on it. This sort of interaction mainly occurs with older people; usually I just brush it off with a smile.

As I get older, though, I am noticing the way that language occupies a space of power, and becoming more aware of how my own reluctance to speak Hindi as a child was in many ways a reflection of the cultural hierarchy I grew up with. In fact, language is the most apparent site for the constant tug of war in my life between Australian and Indian cultures.

When my family arrived in Australia, my siblings and parents were already fluent in English because it's the national language in Fiji, spoken in public, at work and in schools. I was only three when we came here, so I learned English from *Play School* and *Sesame Street* – to this day, I can't recite the alphabet without ending on an American 'zee'.

Once I learned to speak English, I basically never shut up. My kindergarten teacher told my parents that she firmly believed I could talk underwater. My rapid-fire speech was linked to my obsessively imaginative mind, which meant I was trying to relay several stories to several people at any given moment. At home, this swiftly went from being cute to being a little alarming.

In fact, my parents were troubled to see that all four of their children preferred to express themselves in English than in Hindi. My parents were already taking a big risk in raising their children in a country far away from their roots. They didn't want us to lose the very essence of our Indian identity, our mother tongue. We all learned to speak Hindi as our first language, even though English was what my parents spoke at work and my siblings spoke at school. But at home Hindi was the norm. In Australia my father implemented a rule: there was to be no talking at the dinner table unless we spoke Hindi. While my siblings adjusted to this rule relatively easily, I remember sitting mutinously silent some evenings after being cut off midway through a story and told to retell it in Hindi.

I tried to explain to my parents that I just felt I could *express* myself better in English. I don't think I could have found a more offensive way of putting it. Much like I assume our colonisers did, I too felt that Hindi lacked the effortless grace and sheer usefulness of English. Of course, the reality was that I was spending the majority of my time surrounded by English speakers, and at just six years old it took a lot of energy to switch into Hindi. While it's easier to learn a language as a child, it's hard to force yourself to use it, unless there's an obvious benefit to doing so. Gradually, I began to respond in English when my parents spoke to me in Hindi, a habit I still have to this day.

The older I got, the harder it became to twist my tongue around the rolled *r* and soft *th* sounds of Hindi. Soon, I became self-conscious when speaking to my cousins, aunts and uncles in Hindi, aware of their amused grins at my accent, and my inability to finish a sentence without slipping back into English. Occasionally, Mum or Dad would interject to correct my pronunciation or language use while I was speaking. As a sensitive teenager, I would refuse to continue speaking after these disruptions, and soon began associating Hindi with feeling awkward or confined.

This fraught relationship has continued to this day. I am still too embarrassed to speak Hindi often, even though I now feel a yearning for my mother tongue. This pull is tied to the deeper sense of loss I often feel in relation to my cultural heritage. It is a loss of legacy, the legacy of my parents and ancestors. Language is the ultimate gatekeeper of cultural identity. Can I truly own my Indian self if I can't speak the native tongue? Can I ever fully connect to my past and to my ancestors without being able to engage with the language they expressed themselves in, both internally and externally? If I don't speak Hindi, don't eat or cook Indian food, don't dress in Indian clothes and rarely practise the traditions I was raised with, can I lay claim to an Indian identity? I have somehow managed to inherit the loss, the experience of prejudice, the disadvantage applied to my heritage without also inheriting the strong sense of identity and nationhood.

For me, language is inherent to identification. I listen to my sisters sometimes as they switch so comfortably between English and Hindi. I think this difference between us comes from the same place that means that they are generally more at ease with their cross-cultural identity while I constantly grapple with mine, unable to view the whole tapestry of who I am without immediately reaching forward to pluck a thread loose.

But it is also the result of a lifetime of having my view of myself troubled by the gaze of others. Language is as much a tool for expression as it is a weapon of limitation, depending on how it is used.

The racism my family and I have experienced in Australia is most often underpinned by the assumption that my family lacks proficiency in English. Most often, when someone has shown open derision towards my family when we're in public, it is in a way that implies they assume that we can't speak English. Sometimes, cashiers will adopt a condescending tone and speak loudly or slowly to us, as though convinced that we will respond in stutters and a heavy accent.

There is a western imperialist attitude to language that does not question the assumed superiority of English, or that a lack of proficiency in it limits the speaker not just in a functional sense but in an intellectual one too. This is obviously the narrow-minded view of a cohort of people, supported and perpetuated by the history of colonialism and the ensuing dominance of English speakers as a result of the genocide, slavery and violence inflicted on colonised cultures across the world.

The outrage expressed at the audacity of a foreigner to arrive in Australia without fluency in English is rarely offered with any self-awareness. The same people who vocally support the idea of a language test as part of citizenship applications are likely those who flock to Bali every summer and shout their cocktail orders in fast-paced English, feeling entitled to expect respectful understanding from non-white staff in a country where English is not the primary language, while offering none in return when the situation is reversed.

Like most people, I do find it challenging to talk to people who communicate differently from me. But I also carry with me a sense of internalised shame that is awoken when I am travelling and unable to express myself in the language of the country I am in.

In Australia, proficiency in English is not just taken to signal cultural identity and background – it is also seen as a marker of intellect. Regardless of a migrant's actual intellectual capacity or occupation, if they are unable to speak English entirely correctly, or if they speak with a strong accent, they are often assumed to be less intelligent. I have regularly seen this assumption play out in regard to my parents. Both speak fluent English but with a slight Fijian accent, and I have seen white staff at restaurants labour over the basics of menus with them as if they can't read.

I have also seen it in my professional life. Once, an organisation I worked for was attempting to develop an internal communication strategy to let staff know about a major structural change in the organisation. One well-meaning white staff member spoke at length about how important it was to ensure the language in all communications was simple and the concepts weren't too complex, because many of her staff had English as a second language.

I interjected to suggest that we have all the relevant communications translated into the primary languages that our staff spoke in addition to English – we didn't need to dumb the content down, we just needed to make it available in other languages. An inability to understand English doesn't imply that the individual can't understand the concepts being communicated – language is a tool, and the ability to use English comfortably says nothing more about a person than that they were raised in an environment where speaking English was important.

Despite understanding the misconceptions that lead to prejudice against non-native English speakers, it's frustrating to be on the receiving end of such racism, given my proficiency in English, knowing that any prejudice I experience is down to my skin colour alone. This discrimination does have a real impact on migrants in Australia. It can affect our employment prospects, educational outcomes and social inclusion.

Unconscious bias on the part of teachers at one of the primary schools I attended meant that I spent almost a year languishing in an English as a Second Language (ESL) development class and missing out on learning another language with the rest of my cohort. At my first primary school, in Albury, I had won the overall academic achievement award for my grade for two years straight, and had passed tests allowing me to transition into a special accelerated stream for children performing at a higher level than average. When we moved to Canberra my parents enrolled me in a public school with a fantastic reputation, in an affluent suburb. I can still remember our tour of the school when we visited Canberra ahead of our move. The teacher showing us around was a big man, tall enough that my father had to tilt his head back to meet his gaze.

On my first day at my new school the following year, the other children in my class split up to study either Spanish or Indonesian, while I was escorted to a small classroom in a distant part of the building. A number of children, of a range of ages and ethnicities, sat around a cluster of desks covered with picture books and flashcards. To my recollection, no one explained why I was joining this class, but I sat patiently with the others while our teacher introduced herself and proceeded to run through basic reading and writing tasks, introducing grammar and elementary English vocabulary in laborious detail.

At this point, I was reading several years above my age level and hadn't touched a picture book since kindergarten. It never occurred to me to question my attendance, because I liked the other children and my teacher, and enjoyed listening to stories and the generally comfortable atmosphere. Of course, it was a massive pain for the teacher to try to accommodate me as well as the other children, given our vastly different language levels. Most of the other children were from diplomats' families, and would be in Australia for a few years at most. Many were fluent in spoken English, but needed extra support with syntax and grammar.

This went on for at least a term. At one point, I was enrolled in both ESL and extension classes for English at the same time. My parents, as far as I know, weren't aware that this was happening (and I sincerely doubt it would have continued if they caught wind).

My inclusion in ESL classes was clearly the result of a reliance on assumption over analysis by whoever sorted out class assignments. Yes, I was born outside of Australia. Yes, I learned English as a second language. But it was also clear to anyone talking to me or reviewing my academic record that in fact I excelled at English. I could have done with some additional tutelage in maths, or physical education (I still have no hand–eye coordination), but English was really not my problem area. Placing me in ESL was not only detrimental to my own education, it was also detrimental to that of the other children in the class, as well as problematic for the teacher.

The fact that the basis for students being placed in these developmental classes (which are a really useful resource for those who actually need them), was our migrant status alone seems unacceptable to me. Immigrants are not one homogenous group. Different individuals will have varying levels of proficiency in language, and their citizenship status can't adequately provide the information needed to best support migrants. Regardless of how well I actually spoke English, my skin colour, my ethnic background and my citizenship history meant that my need for extra tuition in the language was assumed.

In fact, every Fijian citizen is educated in English, and all ordinary business is conducted in English. It is an aspect of our colonial history that has continued to serve as a common ground between indigenous Fijian and Fijian-Indian populations. Based on this, my need for ESL classes should have automatically been discounted, as my country of origin also prioritised the English language.

I could cope with the English-as-king attitudes of some a little better if people made even the barest amount of effort when using words from other languages that have been adopted into English. I am constantly bemused at the way in which Indian words are appropriated without any attempt to understand their true meaning.

I felt a tingling sense of validation when I read Nikesh Shukla's essay 'Namaste' in the collection he edited, *The Good Migrant.* In it, he points out the underlying racism of white people misusing appropriated Hindi words. He writes, 'Namaste means hello . . . It has become a bastardised metaphor for spiritualism.'[9] He goes on to satirise the way white yoga aficionados like to whisper the word at the end of a session, as if the term is somehow sacred and connects them to a higher power. This practice has always annoyed me when I go to yoga classes. I feel irritated every time a white yoga instructor wearing *kurta* as pants (which, by the way, is like wearing your underwear on the outside in my culture) stares at me as the lone Indian in the class and says 'Namaste' in a whispery voice, with a benevolent, meditative smile on her face. I want to yell 'G'day to you too!' but I limit my rebellion to not saying namaste along with the rest of the class.

I do yoga for exercise. It's nice if people find it relaxing for the spirit and the mind. But why not do your research? Understand the words you're saying? It would be more meaningful to just say 'thank you' or 'well done' at the end of a class.

In the same essay, Shukla writes about how the most common argument he has with people about language revolves around something as simple as tea. 'Chai means tea. Chai tea means tea tea. The number of times you see this on a menu makes you wonder why people can't be bothered to do their research.'[10] This is another of my pet hates.

I don't care if people enjoy cultural artefacts from Indian culture – in fact, India quite happily exports yoga and chai to the western world for an economic benefit. Do as much yoga and drink as much chai and eat as much curry as you like. I genuinely enjoy being able to share these wonderful aspects of Indian culture with my friends, and to be able to enjoy them in Australia, as far as we are from the country where they originated. But surely if you're using words from another language, it's worth learning to use them correctly. The laziness with which the western world misuses borrowed Indian words implies the disregard it has for other cultures. God forbid a migrant uses the wrong words in English while on Australian soil, but white people can happily order their 'tea teas' and their 'bread breads' (naan just means bread, you guys), and no one can ever call them on it.

It's similar to the number of times I have introduced myself to a white person only for them to roll their eyes and insist on calling me 'Zoe' instead of just learning how to pronounce my phonetically spelled, four-letter name.

As a younger and less confident person, I used to agonise over how to say a fellow Indian migrant's name when in the company of our white friends. They all pronounced it incorrectly, and other people took it for granted that their mangled version was his actual name. I knew the correct pronunciation but didn't want to make him uncomfortable by being the only person to use it. It annoyed me to think that not a single white person bothered to check their pronunciation.

I worked with two South Asian women for many years, both of whom had phonetically spelled names. Yet not a single white staff member ever pronounced their names correctly – sometimes the names were unrecognisable. No one took a moment to ask either woman how to pronounce her name and then commit it to memory. I made a point of saying the names correctly, and of correcting my colleagues, but it didn't seem to make an impact. I even overheard some colleagues complaining about how hard it was to say the women's names.

As a migrant, I do not have to feel grateful to the millions of white people in Australia for my right to be here. I do feel gratitude to and empathy with Indigenous Australians, as a beneficiary of their violent experience of colonisation. I have no obligation to accept the easier versions of my name that I am offered when people don't want to learn to pronounce it properly. I should not just be glad they're trying to say it at all, or accept that it's 'hard' for people to pronounce, as I have been told before.

The supremacy of the English language is a lasting effect of a colonial history built on violence, slavery and the rending of multiple countries and their cultures. If the one thing the descendants of the perpetrators of colonialism are asked to do is to use their mouths to form non-English words and non-Anglo names in as correct an approximation as possible, this is a small, insignificant thing.

And if you consider yourself a progressive, culturally inclusive individual, don't feel embarrassed and unable to ask how to pronounce the names of the POC you meet. Ask, and try to form the rolled *r* or the soft *th* sounds of an Indian name, and I will forever see you as an ally.

The place of language in my identity has changed significantly over the years. As a child, I was delighted by words, always desperate to capture them on the page, and I felt Hindi slowed me down, made my words sluggish and uncertain, whereas in English they flowed freely.

Yet as my connection to Indian culture grows more tenuous, no longer automatically passed on through my parents but instead requiring effort and constant engagement from me, language has become a central concern. Language is in fact the stitches that hold together a cultural identity. I can wear the clothes, eat the food and visit the physical sites of my Indian heritage, but without a strong grasp of Hindi, my experiences will be muted, black and white to the local Indian's technicolour.

Language is not just the site of cultural ownership, it has often been a site of cultural oppression. In the destructive processes of colonisation, language is often the first tool through which native cultures are erased. The forced removal of Indigenous Australian children from their parents, to be educated in white schools and fostered into white families, is one example of this; the ban on using the Gaelic language after the Jacobite uprisings in Scotland is another. Language is inherent to identity, and to silence it is to stopper the flow of cultural inheritance at the spring, pulling each generation further away from their ancestors.

My disconnect from Hindi, my awkwardness when speaking it, is just one more example of the ways in which Australia has cloaked my Indianness. Worse, the next generation will be even further removed: my nieces and nephew are growing up more Australian than even I was, with less proficiency in Hindi. This is inevitable. It is part of generational migration. It is as much a sign of my parents' success in achieving a 'better' life for their descendants as it is a thorn in their side.

How strange it must be to have to communicate with your own children and grandchildren in the language you are second-most comfortable in, to speak a language other than the one you think in. How bizarre it must be, over decades, to switch between two languages so often that facets of one leak into another. (My family often add *-ing* to Hindi verbs, and we speak a 'Hinglish' at home that we don't even realise is not fully one language or the other.)

I wonder if my parents ever regret their migration for this reason. I know that my father, in particular, worries that his grandchildren won't be comfortable speaking Hindi, and he still tries to nudge them to speak the language when at home (with little success). Like mine, their tongues can fly so quickly in English, whereas Hindi feels laborious. My parents are the opposite – even though they are fluent in English, it is in Hindi that they have the most elegance with their words. I imagine that, for them, speaking English is a conscious process, like holding your breath underwater, whereas speaking Hindi is like having the gills of a fish and being able to swim effortlessly. I can sense their joy and freedom when they converse with family and friends in Hindi, the old notes and rhythms of their conversation flowing out easily and swiftly.

For me, every word is an effort, every phrase thought out before I utter it. Lately, when sitting in traffic, I sometimes find myself trying to say a sentence in Hindi and stumbling over the structure, unsure what preposition to use. When older family members visit us and I know they will expect me to speak in Hindi out of respect, I stay mostly silent, communicating with smiles and nods. My discomfort mirrors the uncertainty of generations of immigrants in western countries, adopting a polite, nervous smile when navigating the hostility of locals to non-native English speakers.

Even as I grieve for my Hindi, I am grateful for my English. I am pleased at my ability to arrange words on a page in a way that expresses my thoughts better than speech ever could. I am proud when commended on the swiftness of my speech, the way my accent is uniquely Australian. But this pride is a result of a global system that is based on the assumed superiority of English and English-speaking cultures. It is odd that the majority of the world's population is either Chinese or Indian (noting that those terms can hardly encompass the diversity of cultures encapsulated by them), yet the languages of these countries are not given equivalent weight in international systems.

And on a personal level, I feel the erasure of my Hindi as both a micro and a macro issue. As a migrant, I am always grasping the cliff edge of inclusion with just my fingertips. But the price of inclusion is culture, and language is often the first thing to go. If I am travelling with my family for more than a few days, the language floods back into me, the words often appearing just moments before I need them. The connection doesn't last, though, and once I am back to my usual routine, my Hindi becomes rusty again.

I don't want to lose this connection to my culture, and to my parents. As studies have shown, immigrants often revert to their first languages as they grow older, and I can already see how this may happen with my parents. When they are old, I want to be able to sit with them and record their stories and memories in the language they are told in. I want to harness the beauty and cadences of Hindi, the simultaneous formality and playfulness it displays. I want to teach my children the foundational words of the language so they can hold small nuggets of our origins within themselves, even when their own selfhood will be founded in our adopted home. Language can be like a map, with detours, broken roads and missing links, but the essential pathways captured safely, to be used again and again, without ever truly being eroded. I want to keep the path clear and navigable for myself, and for those who come after.

THE 'SLUMDOG' REALITY – CONFRONTING POVERTY IN INDIA

Travelling to India from a first-world country is a culture shock, no matter what your background is. The first time I set foot on Indian soil I was eleven years old. We were visiting for eight weeks, and I had been dreading it. I remember complaining to my friends at school that if it was anything like Fiji, I wouldn't enjoy it.

I always struggled when we travelled to Fiji during the summer holidays – the humidity and chaos of Suva exhausted me, and I missed Australia, homesickness gnawing at me like a toothache. I expected India to be the same, only amplified. I was completely unprepared, then, for the deep love and sense of belonging I felt when we finally arrived in Mumbai. Yes, it was overwhelming and chaotic, like Fiji, but it's difficult to explain the beauty and immensity of India without relying on cliché. Everything is different, and the pace of life is about three times faster than in Australia. It fascinated me to see the country that my ancestors came from, to walk along its streets and feel I was somewhere I belonged, where the complicated tangle of my heritage actually began.

Before we travelled, I had overheard snippets of conversation between my parents and their Australian friends who would visit for dinner. They often discussed the measures tourists could take to protect their personal items, and how one could avoid the attention of beggars. I didn't understand this – to me, beggars were those harmless, sad-looking men who sat against dirty shop walls in Garema Place in Canberra, staring dejectedly at the ground, with an empty coffee cup in front of them for coins tossed their way. These men barely acknowledged the flurry of feet that stomped a path in front of them, let alone made any kind of threatening movement that passers-by needed to avoid. I couldn't imagine how they could pose a threat.

Already anxious about our trip, child-Zoya didn't dwell on these brief hints of poverty in India. The country in my parents' stories already seemed too vast to understand or contain. My imagination reeled when they described the bustle of the cities and the sheer size of India, how different it was from tiny Fiji. Leaving home for any length of time always stressed me out – I was quite opposed to change as a child, and our trips were fast-paced and immersive. My parents liked to really travel, to get into the gritty underbelly of the countries we visited and wring the most out of each day. This was usually fun in practice but terrifying in prospect. Add to that the sheer distance (it was the longest flight I had ever been on), and I was more than a little nervous. In retrospect, I wish I had asked my parents to explain it to me then, to give me some context to understand the inequality in India – as it was, the sudden exposure to a city soaked in abject poverty was a harsh awakening.

When we finally arrived in Mumbai and left the airport, the six of us and my grandmother in two taxis driving in convoy, it was like entering a tornado. I clutched my mother's hand, caught between awe and fear as the taxi careened through the streets. Cars drove everywhere on the road, without any semblance of order. Motorbikes zipped past us with entire families crammed onto them, women riding elegant side-saddle, their *dupatta* scarves pulled over their mouths to filter out exhaust fumes. The cacophony of horns beeping and voices shouting was set against the backdrop of a city teeming with activity. Carts lined the streets selling everything from cooked food and raw vegetables to knick-knacks and clothing, and buildings rose above us in crooked formations.

Beggars were everywhere – there were men without legs, pulling themselves along the street on makeshift skateboards. There were small clusters of people covered in oozing sores and boils – what I later discovered was leprosy – shunned by all who passed them. There were small children missing eyes or limbs, or with acid burns twisting the skin of their faces. Some people were just one step up from beggars – children collecting plastic and glass from the sides of the road to sell to the recycling plants for a handful of coins; girls walking between cars with cheap flowers wrapped in flimsy plastic, selling to white tourists; men sitting in doorways with shoe-shining kits, their eyes blank as they rubbed the black leather of a richer man's shoes until they could see their own circumstance reflected back at them.

We were in Mumbai for a few weeks, and my parents had warned me that our time in the city would probably be the most difficult in terms of daily confrontations with beggars. After that we were going to rural Gujarat, where there were fewer street beggars. I soon felt anxious every time we walked down a crowded road lined with ragged forms with hands outstretched. It was very hard to walk past these people and know that we couldn't help everyone. It made me feel cold and heartless, but if we had given one person a handful of rupees we would have been mobbed. Because of our skin colour the beggars usually left us alone, assuming we would be well-versed in the cold-shouldered, blank-faced approach of other locals. But as soon as someone heard us speak – especially if one of us children forgot the golden rule to always speak in Hindi (to avoid being rorted by taxi drivers and other vendors once they realised we were tourists) – we would be thronged with desperate hands and pleas for money.

There were other markers of our difference than just language, of course. Our clothes were a little distinctive, our Hindi accents strange. One shop owner told my mother that he knew she was from overseas because she hiked her trousers up slightly as she walked through the dirty streets, to avoid getting cow manure on the hems. 'Mumbai people don't care about this,' he told her.

Even though we were surrounded by shades of skin colour that mirrored our own, I couldn't help feeling that Indians in India were gleefully anticipating the moment when they could point to us and say, 'Ha! See – you're not really Indian!' It was as if they wanted to demonstrate that our achievement in migrating to a first-world country came at a price – the loss of our very *Indianness*. We now spoke differently, walked differently, dressed differently. We cared about such trivial stuff as manure clinging to our trousers, when real Indians had far greater concerns. I hated these moments. I hated the constant reminder that while I didn't fit in in Australia, I also didn't fit in here, the idealised homeland. Even in Fiji, surrounded by other Fijian-Indians, we were starkly aware of the indigenous Fijian population and knew that our presence there wasn't strictly 'natural' – we were immigrants first, not the true custodians of the land. India was meant to be different, the one place in the world where we were meant to belong, so any indication that this wasn't the case niggled at me.

Yet I still felt something of a homecoming in my bones from the moment we arrived in India. My whole life I had called myself 'Indian', used this term to signify the core of my identity, and yet I had never laid eyes on the land itself. There, in Mumbai, I could almost see the faint lines in the earth mapping the journey that my ancestors took from their lives here, all the way to my own life, undeniably foreign to theirs, but the outcome of their labour. In the people we saw toiling at their businesses and ventures, I saw the tenacity and work ethic that people so often associate with Indian culture. I could also see the richness of the environment – from the lush forests on the outskirts of the city where we visited relatives, to the busy beach of Juhu, where the Ferris wheel lit up every night, always a party without any occasion to celebrate. Here was the depth and colour and vibrancy that I had only previously glimpsed in the artificial world of Bollywood, come to life in reality. It was overwhelming, and sometimes exhausting, the pace so different from the placid streets of Canberra, but I also loved it, the novelty enticing to my child's eyes. The only thing tarnishing my sense of wonder was the poverty I saw all around me.

Beggars were not the only sign of India's massive inequality and low living standards. When we travelled into Gujarat, to the villages where my grandparents were born, the poverty was less confronting, but still undeniably there. The villages are in more rural areas, like small towns but with a stronger sense of shared identity. In India, your home village is as important within the state as the state that you're from is within the broader context of India as a country. It's funny to think how irrelevant the title word 'Indian' really is to people in the country, where each state has a different dialect and culture, and villages or towns within each state have their own localised customs as well. I never had a clear idea of how many kilometres my grandmother's village, Hinglot, spanned, or the population size. But it functioned like a town, with its own school and small economies.

The red dirt road leading into Hinglot was lined with flowering bushes that waved purple blooms in greeting as our hired four-wheel drive rolled down the road, bringing us to our ancestral home. Tears sprang to my grandmother's eyes when she saw it. She had moved to Fiji after her marriage, and only visited India a few times since, when funds allowed. The gaps between trips spanned many years, but each visit back was a reconnection to the core of who she was – a Hinglot citizen first, then Gujarati, then Indian, then Fijian-Indian.

Her brother, Ahmad, now lived in England but still had a home in Hinglot, where he spent several months of the year with his wife, Biban. The family had another house, where my grandmother's sister-in-law Fatimah tended to her mother, whom we called Par-Dadi (great-grandmother). Par-Dadi was as brown as a nut, her skin clinging to her skeleton, and with lines as deep as rivers running down her face. She grinned at us toothlessly, and spoke in Gujarati, which I only vaguely understood. Still, her pleasure in seeing her great-grandchildren was evident.

Both the houses were double-storey and had gated yards with gardens. By contrast, most of the other dwellings in the village were squat, single-storey homes with lumpy walls painted bright-blue. Watching family groups sitting outside, the mothers methodically picking through the daughters' hair, I asked my mother what they were doing. 'They're picking out lice,' Mum told me. At the time, I couldn't understand why they didn't just buy head lice shampoo.

I had little understanding of economic inequality at that age. Beggars, I understood, with their ragged clothes and dirty skin, the hollow look in their eyes as they asked for money, as if mentally they had already anticipated our rejection and moved on. But this kind of inequality – where families had homes, even if they all slept in one room, and they had food, even if they all ate from a single plate – confused me. How did their circumstances exist in the same street as my family's, whose houses had multiple rooms, and real kitchens, and entire gardens? What stroke of luck or fate had made my family's lives so markedly different, even in India, from those of the women who worked for my great-uncle? I understood my own immediate family's difference as migrants who had managed to reach the fabled shores of the first world (a dream for many Indian people), but that people living in such close proximity could have such diverse living conditions was harder to comprehend.

The sight of women working as servants in my great-uncle's home was the most confronting aspect of the class hierarchy in India, something I only understood in retrospect as I grew older. Two women, Mariam and her sixteen-year-old daughter Mumtaz, worked as maids for my great-uncle and great-aunt. Every morning, I would lazily stumble out of bed, brush my teeth and trail down the staircase to the kitchen. Mariam and Mumtaz would already be hard at work – doing laundry, and making roti and curry for us to eat.

My great-aunt was always working with them. I observed all three women with fascination, intrigued by the tasks they carried out using strange utensils that we didn't have back home, but I was especially interested in Mariam and her daughter. I didn't fully understand their connection to the family, but I was impressed by their confidence and the casual way they undertook tasks that would have exhausted me, like hauling laundry outside, and cooking meals for at least ten people at a time. Mariam had a way of tucking her headscarf behind her ears so that she wouldn't overheat. I thought it looked funny, but I also admired her practical, no-nonsense approach to the back-breaking work. Food was mainly prepared on mats on the ground. We also ate on the floor, as a family, sitting in a circle.

I felt uncomfortable eating with Mariam and Mumtaz working nearby, having started the day much earlier than us. My Australian egalitarianism made it difficult for me to allow them to serve me food or wash my dishes. They weren't treated entirely as servants, but they were still employees, and their role was still to keep us, as the guests, comfortable. In Australia, I was used to everyone in the family pitching in around the house; only the very rich had personal employees.

Of course, I can now see that a culture of servitude exists in Australia, but it's cloaked in a sense of capitalist equal opportunity, where we pretend that all waitresses and checkout assistants are serving us out of complete choice in their employment, unaffected by inequality in access to education or opportunities. In India, though, servants aren't just the people in uniforms in restaurants or behind the counter. They are women and men who spend more time with their employers than they do with their own families. Children, too, are taken out of school to work demanding jobs that will contribute to the family's income.

Mumtaz was a pretty, bright girl. To me, she was the ultimate example of a cool teenager who was smart and funny, and also gorgeous – young men burst into snatches of Bollywood ballads when she walked past the village shop. She took my sisters and me out to the local Eid festival celebrations, showing us around the carnival. I remember her grinning face, her hair escaping her headscarf, the way she bossed her younger brothers around. I also remember her explaining that she would be married within the year. At sixteen and in the cultural context, she was already getting too old, and it was important for her family that she make a good match.

'Isn't she too young to be married?' I asked my sister later that evening, after Mumtaz had left us for her own home.

Zaheeda shrugged. 'Not really – sixteen is a grown woman here. It's different from Australia. It's probably hard for them to afford to keep all of their children at home for much longer.' Daughters are seen as more of a burden than sons, as when they marry they join their husband's family and no longer contribute to their own. In rural areas, where ongoing education and job opportunities are more scarce, it makes sense to marry daughters off as soon as they're eligible.

Perhaps I am projecting my own sense of their circumstances onto Mumtaz and her family. But I remember thinking that, at sixteen, I would still be in school, studying, looking forward to university. Marriage would be at least a decade away. Writing this now, I am still unmarried, happily exploring the world with my partner, my independent income and my freedom.

Watching Mumtaz, then just a few years older than Zaheeda, I realised that the distance between our lives was one of more than kilometres, or money, or language. It was the access to sexual education, and the existence of age-of-consent laws that prevent children from being married before eighteen. It was the access to public health programs and government welfare that prevent most Australians from living in poverty. At the time, I felt overcome by gratitude that my life was not like Mumtaz's, and that my world was grounded firmly in western democracy.

Now, of course, I am less naive. I am still glad that I grew up in Australia, but I am also more aware that my attitude towards Mumtaz's situation was founded in a western supremacism that assumes that the things we value should be valued the same way in all cultures. It's impossible for me to say whether Mumtaz was happy with the path set out for her, and whether marriage was a choice or an obligation. But I do know that she loved her family fiercely, that the village was her home and sanctuary, and that when we visited years later she seemed happy with her husband and their first child, then a toddler. Perhaps I had imagined the wistfulness I saw in her at sixteen when she spoke of her impending marriage. Perhaps I projected my own confusion about women's lives in India onto Mumtaz, as she chatted to us in the kitchen, her hands busy kneading dough for roti, or scrubbing clothes in a big basin.

My ancestors had made sacrifices precisely because they wanted their descendants' lives to be starkly different from that of the Mumtazes of the world, even if they perhaps came to regret that departure from the culture that made us. It was a double-edged sword, because the same forces that gave me educational and economic opportunities unavailable to Mumtaz also took from me the sense of familial responsibility and loyalty she had, and the willingness to get married and take on the roles Indian culture expects dutiful daughters to play.

I had assumed that, given the choice, Mumtaz would want economic independence, education, sexual liberation. But what was the cost? The alienation I now feel from the country that made me was a price we paid. The guilt and the loss of selfhood were sacrifices I didn't yet understand at age eleven, unable to see the way my cultural duality as both Fijian-Indian and Australian would be harder and harder to balance.

I still remember the Eid festival that year, the way the sun caught the edges of the rickety Ferris wheel in the field, and the smell of *pakoras* and *jalebi* wafting from the food stalls. I remember Mumtaz's grin, her nose ring glinting in the fading light, and the flash of vertigo I felt, thinking of what my life could have been in another place.

This trip to India was the first time I realised that the uncomfortable clenching feeling in my gut when I saw people who weren't that different to me living in much worse circumstances had a name – migrant guilt. It was the same sensation I had in Fiji sometimes, when other children commented on my clothes or new watch, or were excited to see their image in our digital camera, and I realised that the things I took for granted were markers of privilege in another context. Or when Indians anywhere complimented my English, as if it was something to be proud of.

The sensation of migrant guilt in India soon became as familiar to me as an aching bone or twitch – unwelcome but unavoidable. It also doesn't escape me that in dealing with the injustice of economic inequality, I managed to make the suffering of others somehow entirely about me. The individualism that I learned in Australia was impossible to switch off. We're told in Australia that poverty is a result of personal choices – that people have equal educational opportunities and supposedly equal access to employment, so if they are living on the poverty line it's a case of self-created hardship. Similarly, if we want to help people in those circumstances we can choose to spend our own income in donations to charities. It's a view that makes poverty bite-sized and both everybody's responsibility and nobody's responsibility at the same time. Yes, we have a functioning welfare system, but if you fall through the cracks of it (which years of working in the charity sector have shown me that people do, and for many different reasons), your well-being is incredibly tenuous.

But in India, some experiences yanked me entirely out of myself and forced me to confront the immensity of poverty, and the helplessness of the individual. One incident stands out to me from our second trip to India, when I was sixteen. I remember standing on a popular tourist street in Mumbai as my father and our driver discussed the next step of our journey. Across the road, stores were slowly waking up to the day, shutters rolling up and the jangling clatter of work beginning.

My eye was caught by a small boy sitting on the stoop beside a shopfront. He was unkempt and tiny – perhaps three or four years old. His eyes had the same empty expression I had come to recognise in beggar children across the city. This boy looked defeated, his head lowered, his mouth slightly open. On his lap he held a baby, perhaps a year old. She wore a ragged dress, and had a distended belly.

Without stopping to think, I crossed the road towards them. I had a small packet of pineapple pieces in my hand that I had intended to eat as a snack in the car, but before I knew it I was in front of the boy, holding the packet out to him. He took it automatically, nodding his thanks. I crossed the road again, and when I turned back, I saw him breaking the pineapple pieces into small chunks, and slipping them into his sister's mouth, supporting her back with his small arm. I was transfixed. It was such a clear demonstration of the impact of poverty. When I was his age, I could barely feed myself, let alone care for anyone else. But this child had the weary maturity of the disadvantaged.

The sight of his selflessness broke me a little. It is not the sort of image you forget easily, and it reinforces for me that no number of *Slumdog Millionaire* viewings can impress on the western viewer the poverty in India like seeing it in person.

Perhaps the strangest part of witnessing poverty in India was finding myself so clearly on the other side of the fence from the people we saw. To all outward appearances I was Indian, but in reality I was so *not* Indian that even my guilt and concern came to me in a detached way. My guilt had no tangible effect on me or my life, because I could leave and return to Australia and never have to fear that that boy's life would become a reality for me. This realisation was confounding to me as a teenager – that after we left India, this boy would continue to wander the streets with his baby sister, that his life was stretching on and on, not just contained in the brief vignette I witnessed. I took a photo from across the road, and when we got home I pasted it into my journal. Over the years, I have often glanced at it and wondered if he is still alive, and if his situation ever improved.

When I think of my connection to India I have always felt like an imposter. I can dip in and out, whereas real Indians can never leave the realities of their heaving, complex, rapidly changing country behind. Travelling to India forced me to acknowledge both my gratitude at being an Australian citizen, and the way in which the positive connection I had formed to India on that holiday was possible precisely because it was a tenuous one – it could be simple, because I would leave again, and India would remain frozen in time for me until I next visited. For that boy with the pineapple pieces, India was his reality, and his relationship to the country was as ever-changing as our relationship is with the weather or the very air we breathe.

Guilt is a selfish feeling, I now realise. Guilt is my way of responding to the dissonance I feel when I witness lives only a small step removed from my own but that are based in suffering, while mine is based in advantage. When we give to beggars our motive is often as much to relieve ourselves of the discomfort of this guilt as it is to have a positive impact on someone else.

Islam holds charity as a central pillar of faith. Each year during Ramadan, Muslims are required to donate what they can to the needy. My parents always distribute their charity as widely as they can, by putting children in our villages in India through school, and donating large sums to relevant charities that are near our relatives in India. I believe they give so generously as a result of their strong faith and desire to do the right thing, and also because they themselves lived with very little as children and feel a sense of duty to use their success to help others. Charity is also a sort of penance – atonement for our good fortune in living a life without hunger or fear or suffering.

When I donate to someone in need, I hate to think that they might feel obliged to demonstrate gratitude. I want it to be clear that my giving is the bare minimum I should do, as someone who has more. Even as a child, my heart would hammer when I approached someone to offer them a few coins or a low-denomination note. To this day, I can rarely not give money to a beggar, especially in Canberra. I have worked in the charity sector there for too many years to hold the false beliefs people often cite for not giving money to the homeless – beliefs such as 'There's no excuse for homelessness when we have such a good welfare system in place to provide for everyone'. Or, 'If you give them money, they'll only spend it on alcohol or drugs'. These ideas are based on a sort of moral judgement, that suggests that our privilege gives us power in assessing someone else's life choices as worthwhile or not. If I offer money to a stranger, it is not a contract. I don't care if they use it to get high on drugs or alcohol, if that's something that will give them comfort. I don't care if they don't spend it on food or accommodation. It's pointless to assume that there are better or worse ways for someone who is down and out to spend the small amount of money they have, or to expect that your hastily given $2 is going to go into some savings fund to get them out of their situation.

In India, the systems are even more fraught than in Australia. There isn't an effective welfare system for me to point to, as justification that our donations aren't necessary, and there's no way of saying which child or mother or disabled person deserves my money more or will spend it more appropriately. Even though these hierarchies of deserving mean little to me, how can I make a choice between the dozens of outstretched hands, when the money I have to give can only stretch so far?

Giving money to the needy is a fleeting contact with a life I will otherwise never touch, a brief moment when the orbit of my existence and the orbit of theirs touches, before we spiral away again. It's an acknowledgment of their suffering, and of my comfort, and the way that the pendulum could have swung in a different direction for both of us.

In our last week in India on that first trip, my parents took us to a temple area in Agra. There was a huge communal pot of food being stirred with giant spoons in preparation for feeding the hungry. There were poor people everywhere. My father gave each of us children the equivalent of twenty Australian dollars in rupees and told us to find someone to give it to. It was our choice, he said, but he encouraged us to think about who needed it the most, and where it would have the biggest impact.

I took a long time to choose, conflicted and unsure. Eventually, I made my way to an old man slumped against a tree in the courtyard. His gaze was still, his posture one of rest. I don't know why I chose him – perhaps just because he seemed so exhausted that he was unable even to beg anymore, and I felt he needed the help keenly in that moment. I bent down carefully and offered him the note, conscious of not showing it to anyone else for fear of being mobbed. He looked startled, and then reached up to take it. As his hand touched the note, we were briefly connected through the money, and our eyes met. He nodded, and I stretched my lips in an almost smile.

And that was it. I did not feel proud of my charity, or glad that I had 'made a difference'. I just felt hollow, and sad, a feeling that echoes in me every time I see someone suffering now.

When the biggest difficulties I face in my life in the diaspora can never reach a level where I fear for my comfort, safety or survival, I have no right to compare my experiences with those of the actual poor. Those moments in India taught me that, despite my skin colour and ethnicity, I will always have more in common with the white middle class in Australia than with the billions of Indians who live lives that are universes apart from mine. When necessities like hunger and thirst are such pressing concerns, culture is relegated to a lower priority. The things that connect us often have very little to do with who we are, and more to do with how we live.

THE LOVE OF AN ANIMAL

The first time I tried to go vegetarian I was eight. We were living in Albury, in a modern brick house that my father had built with the help of a handful of other men. The ground under the foundations had been our playground for months, as the house slowly went up around us. After school, we would play in the piles of sand and cement in the backyard, the block of land the first thing we truly owned in our new country.

Now the novelty had worn off, and the house was truly a home. We prayed each evening in the front lounge, and sat down for dinner together in the informal dining room, each of us four children trying to beat the others to the prized dining position – in between Mum and Dad.

But tonight, dinner had taken on a newly sinister quality. That day, my father and brother had driven out to a nearby farm and returned with three chickens. I was delighted at our new clucky friends, their sleek feathers soft as silk. But their eyes were wild as each was pulled out of their carrier and into the daylight.

My excitement quickly turned to shock as Mum laid out newspaper and brought out the big knives, and Dad began the process of slaughtering each bird in turn, speaking the prayers and following the process that sanctify meat as halal. I watched the throat of each bird being cut, and its blood falling like a fountain to the dry, dusty ground of our backyard. I was aghast. I kept staring between the knives, and the blood and the quickly growing pile of organs that Mum was collecting in separate bowls – those we could eat, and those we couldn't.

When we sat down to dinner that night, I stared at my empty plate, arms crossed. 'I can't eat it,' I told my mother. 'Dad shouldn't have killed them.'

'How do you think we get all of our meat?' Mum said impatiently. 'If Dad doesn't kill them, a butcher does. Allah made animals for us to eat – don't be silly.'

Rather than comforting me, Mum's pragmatism sent me into a spiral of guilt. I thought about every chicken drumstick and lamb curry I had ever enjoyed, and about the chicken or lamb that died for my meal. I imagine my reaction looked a little like Lisa Simpson's wild-eyed realisation about the origins of meat in the famous episode of *The Simpsons* (the same episode that sparked years of me being tormented by the 'You Don't Make Friends with Salad' song, led by my brother).

For one night and part of the next day, I refrained from eating meat, not wanting to take part in the cruelty any longer. But the next evening Mum put a platter of kebabs on the table, and I slowly reached for them, enticed by the smell of the spicy marinade and the juicy sounds of my siblings tucking in. I mean, a growing child needs protein, right?

This was just the opening salvo of a battle I would fight with myself for the next seven years, until I eventually went vegetarian for good at the age of fifteen.

My impulse to protect animals from cruelty and to empathise with animals to the point where I now can't even conceive of eating meat, and have been trying to go vegan for years (cheese remains my barrier food), is something that has been present since that moment of realisation. It is also something that is far less understood or valued in the context of my culture. In fact, my love for animals and my desire to protect them from cruelty has made me stand out from my extended family and peers (not necessarily in a positive way) for most of my life. Where did this empathy come from, and why did it contrast so starkly with the norms of my cultural heritage?

The first pet that was mine to love was a white rabbit named Snowdrop. The choice of name was an unfortunate one, as Snowdrop froze to death. I'm told I begged for a rabbit. I don't remember this, but it seems highly likely that I would plague my parents' every waking moment with pleas for a pet bunny.

Since childhood, I've always felt as though something crucial is missing when I don't have a companion animal.

Sadly, at six my love of animals was not matched with the necessary skills to care for them. I loved the rabbit, and fed him and helped to clean his hutch. But I didn't have a clear idea of exactly how life worked, and how easily it could be snatched away. Nor did my parents have the time to care for a pet either. One morning, as autumn turned into true winter, my father came to my bedside and gently shook me awake.

'I'm sorry, darling,' he whispered. 'Snowdrop is dead.'

I remember climbing onto my father for a piggyback ride to Snowdrop's hutch. Open to the elements, with no straw to cushion him and absorb his body heat, the hutch provided little shelter for the poor rabbit. His body was stretched out, stiff and icy, as hard as a rock. I stroked his side while I cried. It was my first encounter with death, and the first time I became aware that animals were completely at the mercy of their human overlords. If Snowdrop had been free from his cage, he would have found a spot to burrow down and stay warm. But instead, carelessly forgotten when I climbed into my cosy bed, and with my parents too busy with four human children to remember to move the bunny to our garage, he had died alone, cold and unprotected.

I still feel guilty when I think about this now, and about the death of our budgerigar when my sister forgot to feed him – the thought of that tiny life shivering and starving, chirping and never being heard, makes my heart break in two.

Worse, though, is the fact that most of our childhood pets *didn't* die in our care – they were given away by my parents at one point or another, for convenience. First was Wriggle, the dog I don't remember meeting, my parents' pet in Fiji. I don't know much about Wriggle – just a few blurry photos of a big white dog, whom I always thought was named 'Regal', both because of how he looked and because of my mother's accent. In my imagination, Wriggle was a ball of energy, a loving, wet-tongued, wriggly-tail-wagging hound. When we left Fiji, he went to live on a farm with people we knew. Mum told me that when she visited Fiji the next year and saw Wriggle, he was skin and bones, tied to a stake in the ground. 'They were too scared to feed him,' she told me, her eyes melancholy. 'He shouldn't have gone to them.'

I think of the farmers avoiding Wriggle's searching gaze, his eyes pleading for attention and love. I think of his head slumping down onto his paws, his bones poking through the slack skin of his back, his ribs expanding with shallow breaths until they stopped expanding at all. I feel such a wash of guilt, it almost makes me lightheaded.

It is hard for me to understand how an adult could be afraid of a pet dog. To me, dogs are for ear-ruffling, for wrestling on lawns, for hugging close when I'm sad, for licks on my chin, and panting smiles. The dogs I know have always been white dogs. Not in colour, but in their souls. They are from and of the white culture that has the luxury of taking animals as pets, the ability to feed one more mouth, the option of pointless walks and cuddles just for fun, without the tick-tock reminder that every minute is another few dollars gone.

These dogs are not for the developing countries of my origins. I can't blame the Fijian-Indians who neglected Wriggle, without extending that blame out to my parents for leaving him, to the Fijian economy for not providing better jobs so we could have stayed, to the sugar cane farmers who pillaged this land for its bounty and then left it, to the British colonial forces for wreaking havoc on one homeland after another and then turning away entirely. The dogs on Fiji are presumably descendants of the dogs brought over from other parts of the world, the dogs who came to serve a purpose and were abandoned when they no longer did.

Part of the legacy my family had established in Fiji is the trail of dogs we leave in our wake wherever we go now. In Albury, we had a dog called Benji. I was very young so I have only a faint recollection of curly fur, whimpering during a belly rub, brown eyes seen through the slats in our backyard gate, eager for access to our open arms and clever fingers that delivered a squirm-worthy scratching behind the ears. Then, one day, Benji wasn't there anymore. Years later, I found out that my parents had given him away before we moved to our new house – taking care of a dog while moving into a house that still needed finishing touches wasn't seen as ideal. After Benji was Smudge, a labrador/cocker spaniel cross who was given away when we moved to Canberra; and there were chickens, rabbits, ducks and an old horse, all given away when we moved from a year on a rented farm into the first motel my parents owned. And then there was Rex.

My memories of Rex are like a slow-moving film reel. Fuzzy at the edges, the figures moving jerkily, the smiles flash-perfect and yet somehow distant. We weren't meant to have a dog. Mum was done with pets, and I already had Cindy, a lop-eared white rabbit my dad got for me from the classifieds one weekend, and who had never truly warmed to me. At twelve, I was far more responsible than I was with my ill-fated first rabbit, but Cindy wasn't interested in my pet-minding credentials. She would hide whenever I opened her hutch, and kick at me when I picked her up to put her into her grazer. We eyed each other with a sort of mutual resignation. I had wanted a cute rabbit that I could raise from a baby. And Cindy just wanted to be left the fuck alone.

Years later, while I was away on a school trip, I got a text from my mother telling me that Cindy had escaped and they didn't know where she was. Many years after the fact I found out what had really happened – my father had let her out to show his visiting sisters and, not used to being uncontained, she had fled. A few days later, Dad found her mangled remains; she had been killed by a fox or feral cat.

But Cindy is not the star of this tale. My memories pan away from her disgruntled little face to the big cheesy grin of Rex – a border collie/kelpie cross who stole the hearts of the entire family.

When my siblings saw an ad for puppies in the paper, we started a targeted campaign on Mum, who was alone with us while Dad was travelling for work. We cajoled and wheedled Mum into 'just seeing' the puppies – we insisted there was no obligation to buy one. But when the seller opened his front door and three adorable little muffin-shaped bundles came tumbling down the steps towards us, Mum was a goner. We were all smitten. I'm surprised we only took one.

Rex soon grew from a wriggly puppy with limited bladder control into a regal, shaggy wolf with the markings of a kelpie and the luscious fur of a border collie. He was a uniting force in our household. We all took turns feeding him and taking him for long walks through the bushland that backed onto our suburb. There was nothing more exhilarating than letting Rex off his leash when we reached the fire trails and watching his graceful body sprint off towards the creek, jumping through the tall grass.

Dad was a little miffed that we had made such a big decision in his absence, but it wasn't long before he was sitting on the porch swing at sunrise, the Quran open in one hand and the other wielding a hiking stick that he used to scratch Rex's stomach, while the dog lolled on the ground before him.

Every afternoon when we got off the school bus, Rex would be waiting at the top of our long, steep driveway, his head cocked to one side, his tail wagging in anticipation. He had a roster of different houses he visited during the day, where he undoubtedly got fed far more treats than any dog requires, but he never missed meeting us in the afternoon.

But it was only four years in that house with the huge backyard before we moved again – this time to the second motel my parents bought. We had no backyard at the motel, just a paved courtyard. There was a big park across the street, but even with two long walks a day, Rex was soon climbing the walls. Every few weeks he escaped and ended up at the pound. His eyes took on a wired, stressed look, and it was heartbreaking to leave him every morning.

One day, I came home to find no wagging tail or anticipatory bark. Mum told me they had given Rex away to a friend of Dad's with another border collie and a large property. I can still remember my feeling of loss and denial. A few months later, a videotape arrived showing Rex running around with his new friend; he appeared to have forgotten us entirely. But Mum told me that his new owners had called to ask if something special used to happen every afternoon at around three. 'He just sits at the top of the driveway for ages – you can't call him away,' they explained. It broke my heart to think of Rex waiting, and us never climbing off the bus.

My family still talk about Rex all the time. He is a firm part of our shared history, the pet who had the biggest impact on all of us, even though he wasn't with us for long. Since then, other dogs have come and gone, but it has taken years for me to build such a deep relationship with another animal.

Now, I am sitting in an apartment in Edinburgh, Scotland, on a temporary working holiday with my cat, Bella, at my feet. Her new home is a far cry from the streets of Yass, just outside

Canberra, where she was found as a stray. People's reactions to Bella's big move to Scotland range from incredulous to judgemental. Most people can't understand why Chris and I would spend so much money on a pet, and think it would have been simpler to give her up for adoption. Others think it's cruel to make a pet travel overseas on a long flight. It *was* a huge expense, and is almost doubled for the return journey, but I could no sooner have left her at home than I could have amputated my own limb. In reality, too, Bella's flight was probably far easier than ours – she got several rest stops and play breaks, and arrived a little frazzled but relieved to see us. Now she's even more affectionate than usual, and spends her time running between us for chin scratches and playtime, and falls asleep purring on my legs each night.

While my whole family has always loved our pets, I can see a difference between my parents' approach and my own. Mum and Dad cared about our animal companions, but they would always prioritise our financial future or their own opportunities over an animal. Although we adored Rex, moving to our next motel helped to solidify our financial status, which led to so many other wonderful parts of our lives, like the family trips we took and the farmhouse my parents live in now. I, on the other hand, can never let go of the sadness I feel for the animals we gave away, and I was determined to prioritise Bella's wellbeing in our move to Scotland. Chris and I agreed early on that if we couldn't take her, we wouldn't go. This attitude is miles away from the dominant attitude to animals in Indian culture.

I now understand that the responsibility I feel for animals is a marker of my privilege. My parents were raised in a country where it was hard enough to feed and take care of your family, let alone a pet. In Fiji, having a pet is a sign of wealth, and most animals serve a dual purpose. On my father's family's farm, cats were loved but they also had to work for their keep as mousers. Dogs were guard dogs, while other animals were primarily there for meat, eggs or milk. Moving from that culture to one where animals are treated as individuals and members of the family, and people shell out for special dog food and vet visits and kennels and toys, must require a difficult shift in mindset.

Still, my parents have displayed a great deal of compassion for the animals in our care, though not necessarily in the way I would expect them to. I remember chickens that we raised from chicks one year when we were temporarily living on a farm after moving to Canberra. The night before we were meant to leave for an interstate road trip, a heavy storm left the young chooks sodden and half-drowned. My parents dried them with towels, and Dad literally warmed them up on the stove, gently breathing life back into them. We left them in a cosy straw-filled box, with food, water and a light bulb on to keep them warm. We departed for our trip, unsure if they would make it.

'I was so worried driving back to the house,' Mum told me recently, when we were recounting this tale to Chris. 'I thought they'd surely be dead, and I couldn't bear how sad that would be, especially for you kids.'

But when we opened the door, the chickens greeted us, having leapt out of the box after recovering and pooed extensively throughout our house. We were overjoyed, my parents relieved that their quick action had averted disaster.

When I think of this story, I realise that empathy for animals is an innate feeling, one that is most often revealed in the immediacy of being confronted with an animal's welfare. My parents have this, and I have seen it play out many times – whether through their care for those chickens, or the way we would feed stray cats, or rescue birds with wing injuries from the sides of roads and call wildlife rescue to rehabilitate them.

Where I differ from them, though, is that my parents would care about saving the lives of those half-grown chickens and yet have no qualms about slaughtering them for us to eat when the time came. To them, that is a natural conclusion of our relationship with the animals. For me, it is unthinkable and the reason I don't eat meat. This is the core conflict between how I see animals and how they do, and it is one I have had to confront in challenging ways throughout my life.

My tipping point into a vegetarianism that stuck occurred thanks to the internet. I spent most of my teen years feeling helpless and frustrated about the world's treatment of animals. By the time I turned fourteen, I was printing petition sheets from World Animal Protection on a range of topics, from banning bear bile farming in China to ending bullfighting in Spain, and hovered outside the main doors of my high school every morning, clipboard in hand, seeking signatures. I baked brownies and sold them for two dollars apiece to raise funds, and negotiated with the school to host a mufti day fundraiser so that everyone would have to donate to causes I cared about.

My reputation as a bolshy animal lover landed me in many an argument over fox hunting, kangaroo culls and eating KFC. Men in particular, including my father, brother and uncles, loved to bait me on the topic and then sit back and watch the fireworks. But even as I pushed other people to change their practices, I was still eating meat at our family dining table every evening. My hypocrisy niggled at me, and when I finally read fact sheets on the People for the Ethical Treatment of Animals (PETA) website at age fifteen, I became vegetarian for good.

My parents did what had worked in the past – they accepted my new identity with only mild objections, and proceeded to starve me out. Mum said she was happy to accommodate me in general, but if I wanted vegetarian food, I could make it myself. She was already feeding six people every night, hard enough without taking special requests. I lasted a few weeks on cheese and tomato sandwiches, before I started feeling light-headed at school, and would lie on the couch each afternoon feeling weak and faint. Mum caved immediately, and for the next six years she kept me supplied in vegetable stir-fry, vegetarian lasagne and curries – so many delicious curries.

It is now thirteen years since I first went vegetarian, and I've stuck to it, with only one detour into eating seafood in response to dangerously low vitamin B12 levels. Now, I toy constantly with going vegan. Thinking about the dairy industry makes me feel sick, and I hate myself every time I eat yoghurt or cheese (while enjoying the deliciousness; I'm aware of the hypocrisy). The fate of bobby calves, male chicks, and the hens and female cows that suffer for eggs and dairy are unjustifiable when we are able to access alternative protein sources to replace these parts of our diets. I know this, and I know I have no excuse for still not being vegan when I hold the values I do. But I also know that I am a terrible meal planner and cook, and would have to radically alter my approach to food in order to stay healthy without the fallbacks of scrambled eggs and milk.

Of course, adopting a vegetarian/vegan diet makes me part of the zeitgeist in the west, where a range of concerns (from health to animal rights and the environment) have seen a spate of new vegan/vegetarian restaurants opening in every city. The only times I have had to consider any layers of complexity when it comes to vegetarianism have been in India. I have always felt like vegetarianism is a no-brainer, but it took walking the streets of my homeland for me to see that widespread concern for animal welfare is a sign of a privileged country – and that poverty and inequality are more closely linked to animal cruelty and neglect than I had ever considered.

As I've described, on my first trip to India, aged eleven, I experienced significant culture shock. As well as the human poverty, I was stunned and confronted by the condition of animals. Stray dogs and cats were everywhere, and there was a strong smell of animal faeces at the entrances to the slums. Pigs, cows, chickens all joined the melee, and I was absorbed by the way these animals continued to trudge through the city, finding food where they could, as if resigned to the chaos and lack of care.

One day I was walking down a dusty street in my grandmother's village in Gujarat when I saw a stray dog lying on her side against a wall with four or five tiny puppies suckling at her teats. I walked back to the house, grabbed a leftover piece of roti, and went over to the dog, as her eyes regarded me wearily, exhausted from simply raising her head. I bent down and threw the roti to her, and waited until she seemed relaxed before I picked up one of the puppies. For a moment, I was lost in playing with the little thing, when I heard my mother's voice, slow and tense. 'Zoya, put the dog down, and back away very slowly,' she said firmly. Glancing up, I found myself ringed by worried-looking adults. I was nonplussed – the dog didn't seem aggressive, and the puppies were cute (if riddled with fleas). I only learned much later that rabies was a concern in India.

This experience and my parents' wariness didn't stop me randomly picking up animals, though. A few weeks later, visiting a different village, we came across a goat and her two tiny newborn kids, still covered in blood and muck. Completely forgetting about my new clothes, I stopped and picked one up – there's a photo in one of our albums of me clutching the kid and grinning with delight. The ease with which I approached the animals betrayed my foreign status: coming from a safe, controlled country like Australia, I had no reason to doubt the safety of animals, because rabies no longer exists in Australia, animals are generally contained, and someone is always liable for other people's welfare – there are any number of safety nets in place.

In India, I only had to glance away from the dog to see hungry-looking maidservants walking along the street, their ribs as stark underneath their saris as the dog's. And if I had looked past the mother goat, still exhausted from giving birth, I would have noticed the tense expression on the face of the man tending to her as he made sure that both kids were alive – the survival of all three goats was integral to the wealth of his family.

When we travelled into Rajasthan, in the north of India, every few kilometres we would see a dishevelled mob of people wandering up the side of the road, often with a horse in tow and one or two bears. The bears, small and brown, looked dejected. The only time I saw one up close, I could see the inflamed hole where its snout had been pierced for a rope to be pushed through. The handler jerked the rope, and the bear reared onto its hindlegs and waved its arms in pain – this was the 'dancing' that tourists paid to witness. My father gave the man some money but told him not to make the bear dance.

I was furious when we got back into the car. 'I can't believe they would do something that cruel,' I fumed. 'How could you give them money?'

Dad sighed. 'They have no other trade – they're like gypsies, travelling from place to place to make money from tourists. He was probably taught to do that by his father, who was taught by his father, and so on.' At the time I thought this was a poor justification, but now that I am more aware of how complex poverty can be, I see how bears (and monkeys, and elephants) become the financial assets of the few men brave enough to catch them. I still don't think it's justifiable, but I also see how my anger needs to be directed more widely than at the individuals who capture these wild animals in the first place, to the systems that make it impossible for them to rise out of poverty without relying on these archaic and cruel practices.

We took a ride on an elephant when I first visited India as an eleven-year-old (something I refused to do when I returned as a teenager, and that I would never condone or partake in again), and afterwards I stood near the great beast's face and watched moisture leak endlessly from her eyes. I know it's a stretch to say she was crying, but the picture was one of complete dejection, and my heart quivered inside me at the sight.

The sadness and anger I felt during that trip every time we saw another skeletal dog or cat scavenging in garbage piles, or watched a man casually whip a horse as it lumbered along pulling a heavy cart, or heard the shrieking, almost human cries of wild pigs as they were hunted and stabbed in the streets of the village, in time became a cold fury.

When I returned to Australia as a sixteen-year-old, my interest in animal welfare took on a new intensity. But for the first time, I could see both sides of the issue. I now understand how India and other developing countries are so far behind the developed world when it comes to animal welfare. For example, the United Kingdom used to allow bear baiting, a practice that was phased out over many years, as a result of a post-industrial society where there are more opportunities for gainful employment, and government-supported welfare. In India, to prioritise the life of an animal could mean choosing the fate of that creature over the fate of your family. A similar situation exists in Fiji, and I understood why my parents felt differently to me on this issue, and on so many others, by virtue of the privilege they had managed to create for me and my siblings. But even with this understanding, the suffering of the animals I saw in India has never fully left my mind.

It was harder for me to maintain my rage and vegetarianism on my second trip to India, at sixteen, when we visited relatives for meals, crowding into their small houses. Despite their poverty, these aunts and uncles and cousins had a quiet dignity and shared optimism that made me feel ashamed of my own casual acceptance of our comfortable lives in Australia. We would sit down on the floor for a meal, and bowl after bowl of curries and condiments would be brought out. When I didn't take any meat, my aunt looked at my mother in concern. 'Why isn't she eating? Is there something wrong?'

Mum glanced at my plate containing only vegetable curries and shrugged awkwardly. 'She eats like a bird,' she said, and changed the subject.

Afterwards, I raised my confusion with Mum. 'I don't get why they were so interested in what I was eating,' I said. 'Should I have tried to take more? I didn't want to be greedy.'

'I know you really care about being vegetarian,' Mum said, 'but it's different over here. They probably only eat meat a few times a year, when they can afford it. They bought that meat in honour of our visit, and it was hard for them to understand why you wouldn't eat it when it was such a sacrifice for them.'

I realised then that at these dinners our relatives never took meat themselves – they encouraged us to eat it, but abstained themselves so there would be enough for their guests. The shame this awakened in me – at the thought of their selflessness, and their poverty, and their confusion as to why I didn't enjoy the result of their labour – meant that for the rest of the trip, I ate what was given to me, choking down meat with a smile.

As I've said, there is no hierarchy of suffering or injustice, but to know that I have the ability to make ethical choices with no adverse consequence to my own wellbeing means that I can't justify turning a blind eye to animal cruelty in Australia. I can make exceptions in the face of such extreme inequality in India, but if anything, this only fuels my determination to advocate for animal welfare when I am back on Australian soil.

I have generally unpopular views when it comes to animal welfare and vegetarianism, views that I know are shared by many fellow veggos and vegans, but that can seem extreme to the mainstream.

I don't believe that you can eat meat and genuinely care about animal welfare. I don't think that there is any excuse for the arbitrary line we draw in the sand when it comes to animals farmed for meat and other products, versus those we choose to love as pets. I think that the only ethical way to eat is to be vegan, and I don't think we have any excuse not to at least be vegetarian.

I don't have this conversation with others very often – it is the exact kind of vegetarian superiority that most people hate about us, and despite my unwavering beliefs, I'm not out to convert anyone. I truly believe that ethical lifestyle choices have to be driven from within, and that people come to these decisions when they're ready.

The most common argument against vegetarianism that you hear from people who do claim to care about animals is that by not eating meat, we're not actually stopping farm animals from being killed. This line of thought argues that to really make a difference, we should lobby for large-scale changes to the farming system to make it less cruel, and in the meantime, there's no point in not eating meat, given that thousands of cows and sheep and chickens are going to die anyway.

To some extent, I can see why people believe this. I don't think that my not eating meat is actually going to stop the farming of animals for food. My abstention from riding elephants in India doesn't stop the legions of tourists who do it every year. My actions are a drop in the ocean, while many people would prefer to be part of the tidal wave of true political change.

I don't pretend to mask my beliefs in rationalism, though, or to be simply guided by the desire for a single outcome. My vegetarianism is motivated by a gut feeling, a bone-deep conviction, that makes me feel sick to consider eating meat. Animals are sentient beings, and I don't think there is any justification for the factory farming processes we use today, which are bad for animals, and also bad for the environment.

I do understand why people feel attacked by my views on animal welfare. It is confronting to consider that you are condoning the systematic abuse and murder of sentient beings. It is much easier to feel disconnected from the meat that you eat, and from the suffering of the animal that died to provide it to you. It is also easy to feel overwhelmed by the sheer magnitude of animal cruelty, and the way it has seeped into so many aspects of our daily lives. When you consider the global meat and dairy industries, and then consider the mammoth effort it would take to stop factory farming across the world, it can definitely fill you with despair. Trust me, despair is a regular emotion for the animal welfare activists I know.

I also don't think that everyone needs to become an animal welfare activist to show that they care about animals – to me, making a personal choice to reduce your own impact on animal farming is a fantastic step, and the most meaningful change people can make. That and donating to relevant organisations that are actually pushing for legislation to end suffering are the best ways to contribute.

I also accept that trying to 'convert' people to vegetarianism or veganism is probably a lost cause. Different causes inspire different people, and although my belief in animal welfare and the rights of animals is unshakeable, I prefer to expend my energy volunteering for organisations that lobby on these issues, rather than personally engaging in arguments with people who are unlikely to change their minds. But I do think that the cultural connotations of caring about animals are hard to suppress. When I donate to animal rescue shelters, or volunteer my time in the offices of OneKind – a leading animal rights organisation based in Edinburgh – I now see it as my duty on behalf of generations of my family in India and Fiji, who have at times treated animals poorly as a result of inequality and poverty and a lack of awareness bred from disadvantage.

I think of Wriggle, and the chicken and sheep slaughtered on my grandparents' farms, the skeletal cows that grazed in nearby fields, the goats killed for my sister's wedding, and the pigs hunted by Sikhs who were paid by our relatives in Indian villages. I remind myself of the huge debt humans owe to the animals who have provided the labour and sustenance that have ultimately built our civilisations.

I think of the cultures that have seen non-white people as no better than animals, as chattels and insentient beings, unable to feel pain or love. I think of how mistreatment breeds mistreatment – the beggar who kicks the scavenging dog, or throws rocks at the pigeons clucking nearby. And I think about the slow-blink my cat Bella gives me when she is lying next to me on the couch, just to express her love for me. I think of Rex, and Smudge, and Benji, and how my parents didn't abandon them, but gave them over to a white culture that prioritises pets because it is able to.

The legacy I bear is one built on a foundation of generations of inequality and abuse. I want the legacy I hand to the next generation to be one that has started taking steps towards a kinder, more compassionate world.

AGAINST THE TIDE

When we walk into the pool area, my shoulders are hunched and my steps timid, unconsciously shrinking away from the water. Chris's hand on my shoulder is both comforting and coercing as he gently steers me to a bench and puts down our towels and sports bag. 'Come on,' he says, his tone light. 'It's not that bad – there's barely anyone here.'

I glance at the pool properly, trying not to gape in dismay at just how long the lanes are. They look endless, stretching off into the horizon. It's an actual Olympic-sized swimming pool – it looks to me like only an Olympian could reasonably be expected to swim the whole length without stopping.

'I really haven't done this in a long time,' I say for the second or third time, looking at him imploringly. 'I'm not sure I even remember how to do freestyle.'

'I'm right here,' he says bracingly, as he pulls off his shirt and snaps goggles onto his forehead. I sigh and follow his lead, awkwardly adjusting my goggles as we walk to the edge of the pool, trying not to feel self-conscious about my wobbly thighs in the new swimsuit.

Chris slips into the water feet first, his body sleek and lean. I do the same, though my entry is less elegant. The water almost reaches the tops of my shoulders.

'So, show me what you would do,' he says.

I shrug, lean forward and do what I think is an approximation of a few strokes, my legs kicking and my arms swooping through the water. As I do this, my body recalls some muscle memory of decades ago and begins to ease into the movement. After a few metres, I pull up and look back at Chris.

'You just swam perfectly,' he deadpans. 'Seriously, I thought you wouldn't even know how to blow bubbles the way you were going on.'

I grin, and acquiesce to the next half-hour of practising.

This trip to the pool is the product of weeks of pleading by Chris. He has seen me through many life-changing experiences over the past six years, including a recent huge change to my health. Some months earlier, I was diagnosed with rheumatoid arthritis, the same debilitating and degenerative autoimmune disorder my mother has. My joints had become sore and achy in the morning, the pain often so sharp it limited my movement for hours. I was no longer able to run, my preferred form of exercise, because the impact left my knees and ankles so sore I couldn't hobble home. Bike riding and swimming were my remaining options, though swimming was pushed as the preferable option by my GP and specialist because it would equally exercise my major joints, and help build lung capacity to improve my breathing at the same time (I also suffer from asthma). We happen to live across the road from a pool, but it had taken me weeks to finally agree to go.

Chris couldn't understand my reluctance to take up swimming. Like all his family, he is completely at ease in the water, and whenever we visit the coast he spends hours surfing. The first time we went to the beach together, Chris had to coax and cajole me, holding my hand as if he could push his own bravery through my skin. Even so, I never went deeper than my waist, and I couldn't muster the courage to dive under a wave, resorting to a less graceful duck every time one crashed over my head.

Over the years since, I have come to a sort of uneasy truce with the ocean. I can enter the water, allow the waves to lift me off my feet and push me backwards, but when I feel the tug of a rip or even a slow drag in the water, my heart hammers and I turn for the shore. It is both the vastness and the unpredictability of the ocean that sparks this fear, and I know I'm not a strong enough swimmer to cope if the worst happened. There's something about the deep ocean, the sense of having nothing but the unknown beneath my feet, that makes me tingle with fear. I want to feel something solid under me, something I can hold onto. There's nothing to hold in the ocean except my own body, and its fallibility.

Once, on our trip to Fiji for Chris's sister's wedding, I allowed myself to be talked into going snorkelling. Everyone else in the group thought snorkelling was a great way to while away the sunny day. But to me, the thought of leaving land so far behind and surrendering myself to the ocean was heart-thuddingly frightening.

Chris's family were kind and encouraging, unaware of the depth of my fear – not surprisingly, seeing as I come from a tropical island paradise. It's a contradiction many people are unaware of – that for many Fijian-Indians, living in a place surrounded by crystal-clear water does not counteract the lack of a beach culture within our lives. Swimming is for those privileged with free time and access to water safety and swimming education; even then, especially in the Muslim community, it is more likely to be available to men than to women.

When I slipped off the side of the boat that day and into the water, my snorkelling mask clamped over my eyes and starting to mist up from my fast, shallow breaths, I realised that I had made a grave error. There is only so much you can fake, and as the white tourists – friends, Chris's family, some strangers – began to snorkel over the coral reefs, pointing out the sights to one another, I drifted in a small panicked circle, my paddling erratic, my breathing strained, looking down past the edge of the reefs into blackness that had no end. Chris and his brothers and nephew held their breath and dived deep, looking like nothing more than humanoid dolphins, cavorting, their bodies lean and powerful. Floundering above them, trying to stay afloat through my fear, I had never felt more aware of how different I was from them.

The Fijian guide saw me struggling, and eventually grabbed my arm, pulling me up to tread water. His hands were on my shoulders, as he told me to breathe, his eyes trying to communicate calm into mine. I let him hold me there, suspended over the abyss, clinging to his arms while my legs kicked out at emptiness beneath me.

Why did the ocean strike such fear in me? Why was I even frightened of swimming pools? Looking back, it's hard to see a cause or trigger in my past.

I started swimming lessons at four or five, the same age as many other Australian children. At the community pool in Albury, I learned to do a mushroom float, to blow bubbles, to dive. I graduated through the classes until I was deemed competent to swim in public pools. And yet I never did feel that competence, always shrinking from water instead of diving in. Why was water, the feeling of immersion, not soothing to me as it was to my peers, but instead filled me with terror? Even as a child, I never looked forward to a swimming lesson.

There was the fact of my skin colour, unmistakeable even through the water, announcing my difference. I was usually the only non-white child in my lessons, and the other children were often unfriendly. Sometimes I glanced over to the side of the pool where my mother sat in one of the blue plastic chairs, her skin the same nut-brown as mine. As she watched me, her posture betrayed some of her own anxiety, her shoulders curled a little in on themselves. We were different in this environment, with nothing to connect us to the white families who gave us a wide berth. To this day, I have never seen my mother swimming, not even wading in water. As far as I know she has never owned a swimsuit, and the thought of her swimming in a pool or the ocean is bizarre to me.

Part of this is grounded in notions of modesty and *pardah*, the Muslim practice of segregating men and women in certain contexts where there is a perceived risk of impropriety. Post-adolescence, swimming in front of male relatives in an Australian swimsuit is unthinkable for the women in my family. We are even embarrassed about being around women who operate outside of those cultural bounds – white women, their skin bare to anyone's eyes – when we're with our uncles or cousins. It's a similar feeling to when someone is fighting at a restaurant table near you, and you flush with the shame you imagine they will feel when they reflect on their impropriety later – I'm ashamed for those women, and equally ashamed at the anti-feminist instinct that is ingrained in me, and ashamed for those men and women who hold onto sexist beliefs about the danger posed by a woman's body, who are not as enlightened as I think I am.

My mother has worn a hijab since her late thirties and always dresses in modest, dignified clothing. I imagine that her lack of interest in swimming is also guided in part by personal preference – she doesn't particularly enjoy physical forms of leisure other than a nice walk, and is happier spending time talking or reading than she would be playing beach volleyball. The idea of a classic Aussie summer holiday at the beach, with boogie boards and bikinis, is alien to my mother, and, by extension, has never felt entirely natural to me. When we did go to the beach in my childhood, we would always have a spectacular picnic, find shells in the sand and make elaborate sculptures. We would enjoy the breeze and the sound of the waves crashing. But our time in the actual water was limited.

All my siblings enjoyed swimming when they did enter the ocean, and it never bothered my sisters to wear t-shirts and long board shorts over their swimmers. They didn't care if they looked different from the white Australian beachgoers, and if their extra clothing weighed them down while they threw a ball in the waves with our cousins, they didn't seem concerned. But I was always held back by these markers of our otherness. I imagined that the people stretched out sunbathing in their tiny swimsuits rolled their eyes at our lack of sophistication, or, worse, pitied us for our religion's emphasis on cloaking female flesh. I flinched when our group seemed too noisy, our calls in Hindi shrieking our difference to the very people I spent the majority of my life trying to fit in with.

Later, going to the beach with friends from university, I found that my childhood anxiety around beach culture had rendered me almost incapable of enjoying myself. Not only did the waves terrify me, but I felt awkward and self-conscious in a swimsuit, unlike my white Australian friends, who seemed at ease in their swimmers at the beach no matter how insecure they might have been on dry land. Something about the beach acted as an equaliser to those comfortable there, but I couldn't relax. I stuck to the shore, walking along the water's edge, drawing in the sand or sitting on a towel a safe distance from the crashing waves.

Even now that Chris's encouragement has made me slightly more confident at the beach, I doubt I would ever enter the water without him. I don't trust the sea, with its strange darkness and ever-changing surface. I don't trust myself to heed the unspoken warnings in the water.

Fear of the ocean is not uncommon in Muslim culture, especially among women. While men may learn to swim for various professions, women are less likely to have the opportunity, and are sometimes banned in the interests of modesty.

In 2004, a Bangladeshi religious group issued a fatwa against women's swimming, causing a local competition to be cancelled. This was tragically ironic, given that on Boxing Day that year a tsunami killed hundreds of thousands of people in the region. In Sri Lanka, over two thirds of the drownings involved women and girls.[11] When I heard this statistic I wasn't surprised, thinking of my own female relatives and how unlikely they were to go swimming. In Fiji, the only time I saw them in the water was at the local river – more of a stream – near my grandparents' farm in Rakiraki, Fiji. The stream served as both a natural laundromat and bath – accompanied by an aunt and female cousin, we would take steel tubs of dirty clothes, laundry soap in chalky white cakes, and plain soap for our bodies. As our mothers pounded the soapy clothes and soap against the rocks that lined the shore, we would sit clothed in the shallow water, rubbing soap up under our shirts, and rinsing it off while lolling in the current.

There were small, white fish that darted around our feet, and we would dry quickly under the burning Fijian sun. It was water, and we were submerged, but it was not swimming. There was enjoyment and playfulness, but not the sort I would associate with the beach in Australia. We would giggle, but it was often with a sense of embarrassment, at our closeness to nudity, at the way our clothes clung to our bodies. Crucially, it was women only – the fragility of our modesty was never forgotten by our mothers.

If Fiji were to be hit by a natural disaster linked with water – flooding, a tsunami – would my female relatives be able to survive? Would their bodies know how to fight the force of water or would they succumb to its depths?

My parents, who have experienced cyclones, coups and uprisings – disasters both natural and unnatural – are polar opposites when it comes to risk. My father has been known to detour off the highway to do a spot of hang gliding, and went skydiving for his fiftieth birthday. My mother is scared of heights, unlikely to dip her toe in water, and prefers the safety of the sidelines to the heady adrenalin rush of adventure. I am more like her than him. To me, water is a risk.

Entering the pool on my own, I feel awkward and more cumbersome than the swiftly moving bodies that pass me. It has taken me days to build up the courage to come here without Chris, but I realise he can't hold my hand forever, and I'm determined to be brave.

There are signs in front of the lanes – I don't even spare a glance for 'Fast' and 'Medium'. Beyond 'Slow' is the even-slower-than-slow lane labelled 'Gentle exercise'. A woman powers up and down this last lane in a well-paced freestyle. For a moment, I glare at her bopping yellow cap, thinking that she does not look like she's gently exercising at all. Then I give up and slip into the water, accepting that I'll have to share the lane.

As I start swimming, my lack of core strength means my legs waver and dip lower in the water than they should, each stroke an effort. Glumly, I think about how strong I was getting before my diagnosis. I was running three times a week, and going to the gym regularly. I was starting to glimpse for myself some of the ease with which Chris moves through the world. He is naturally athletic, running a kilometre in just over four minutes, his calves as hard as rocks.

Exercise has never been a big part of my family life, although my father was very fit as a young man and into maturity. He played squash, went running and enjoyed most sport. Once as a child I insisted on joining him on his run. He patiently led me to the wildlife reserve next to our suburb, our dog Smudge in tow. He parked Smudge and me against a fence, and then ran swift laps from one end of the stretch of fenceline to the other. I was proud of his physicality, and the way it mirrored the athleticism of my friends' fathers, and the sport-obsessed country we now lived in. I never thought about what it must have been like for him to venture onto the squash court in an Albury gym, the only brown man in the building. Or how it must have felt to learn how to play golf, that sport for the wealthy, as an immigrant from rural Fiji. I've never asked my father about that emergence into a white world. He doesn't strike me as someone who has dwelt much on what other people expect him to do or not do. I assume he just strode into this new world with the same audacity and courage he takes into every part of his life.

I wish I had inherited this confidence, but I'm too aware of my own physical inadequacies and differences to be able to relax into using my body for the sheer pleasure of moving. Part of this is down to gender – exercise and physicality are not generally encouraged for women raised in Indian Muslim culture. It's not my parents' fault that I absorbed this message – they encouraged us to play sport and get involved in whatever extracurricular activities we wanted. Between them, my sisters played netball, hockey and volleyball. Some of my friends were forced by their parents to do Little Athletics or join a weekend sports team, but for us it came down to personal choice, and I would always choose to read Harry Potter over heading to the netball courts.

When I joined a gym in my twenties and took up running, my parents were surprised. I was a healthy, normal weight, I had never shown any enjoyment in exercise, and it wasn't a team sport I was doing to socialise, so why do it at all? 'You don't need to lose weight,' my father told me once when I was heading to the gym after a visit.

Later I reflected on his comment. Were exercise and fitness just the pursuits of privileged first-world people with too much time on their hands? I suppose when you're an impoverished woman in an Indian city, carting blocks of concrete balanced on your head from jobsite to jobsite as your only means of earning an income, attaining a beach body is not a high priority. If there wasn't an obvious need to exercise, I could see how it could be considered an odd choice for someone like me who has never claimed to enjoy sport for leisure.

In the water now, I cut a slow line, swimming freestyle, my shoulders already beginning to ache. When I reach the end of the lane, the woman I'm sharing it with is already on her way back. I kick off again, this time doing backstroke, trying to give my lungs a break. It doesn't work – I'm still puffing and struggling. I watch the line of the roof, trying to stay straight. Kicking, swinging my arms, occasionally losing my balance and submerging the top of my head. Then my arms hit an obstruction, and I flail upright. The woman I've just clobbered smiles at me, shaking her head at my garbled apology, and keeps going. I paddle to the side of the pool and pull myself out of the water.

I am embarrassed but not surprised that I managed to collide with the other swimmer. Unable to surrender to the motions of my body, the sensation of being weightless, I am the opposite of graceful in water. As I trudge home, my breath misting in front of me in the winter air, I feel landlocked again, even more aware of my body, and of its inadequacies.

As a teenager, I used every excuse I could think of to avoid our four weeks of swimming in summer physical education classes. I figured I could be menstruating one week, have a note from my parents (forged, of course) excusing me for another, forget my swimmers for one week, and only have to suffer the pool once.

With board shorts and a rash vest over my simple halter-neck swimmers, I looked like an oddly coloured seal, my body swathed and inelegant. After our lesson, most of the girls seemed comfortable undressing in the change rooms; I hunched under a towel as I tried to peel off my wet swimmers and slither back into my school uniform. I would avert my gaze from the older white women who were changing in the open, their bodies marked by the passage of time. Avoiding my friends' eyes, I quickly snapped on a bra, my towel hanging over my shoulders. As much as I hated being in the water, being out of the water was equally bad, and the pool remained a symbol of discomfort.

This self-consciousness is definitely not only the territory of the culturally diverse. I'm certain every teenage girl feels it to some degree, even in the all-female space of a change room. However, my discomfort was not just about my own body but about bodies in general. We never spoke about bodies in my household. There was no talk about the birds and the bees, and nudity was an obvious no-go area. Even when I got my period, it was never fully explained to me at home (thankfully it was all covered in school). I knew that some of my friends had very different upbringings, with parents who talked openly about bodily functions and saw no shame in nakedness. But for me, bodies were the simple scientific drawings in the encyclopaedia, or the clinical talks we received in sexual education classes.

As an adult, I scurry out of the pool complex with my wet swimmers covered by beach pants and my towel wrapped around my shoulders. I don't relax until I'm across the road, back in my apartment, where I can strip off and climb into the shower with no eyes to witness.

Sometimes, looking back, I try to locate the specific moment when my body stopped being a tool I delighted in, one that enabled me to jump on the trampoline or ride my bike, and instead became a source of humiliation. I know weight had something to do with it. I wasn't skinny as a teenager, and I wasn't overweight either – I hovered in that forsaken middle ground, where mean girls rolled their eyes at my chunky hips but I wasn't actually bullied about my appearance.

My distaste for my body was linked to the quiet shame I felt about my skin colour. I never talked about it or examined it closely, but I knew I hated being brown. I would sometimes think to myself that if I could swap my skin for my friends' 'normal' pallor, I would do it without hesitation. When I stripped to swimmers and could see the uneven colouring of my thighs as compared to my forearms, my skin browner where the sun tanned it, and a pale caramel everywhere else, I felt repulsed. The self-hatred was partly that of a teenage girl for the body she is always told is somehow wrong, and partly the discomfort of a person of colour who can't pinpoint why their difference is seen as a lack but unequivocally knows it is not a good thing.

It has always seemed reasonable to me that a migrant might be afraid of new experiences. Growing up in Australia, ever conscious of the ways in which my family was different from my friends' families, I felt justified in my anxiety. I assumed that the unease I felt about things like swimming, wearing shorts in summer or going to concerts was a projection of my parents' anxiety. In my head, they became small figures, shoulders braced against change, reluctant travellers to a foreign land.

In reality, however, their courage was what allowed them to leave behind the poverty and constraints of their childhood and enter the privilege of the first world. As a child, I never understood how strong they had to be to migrate to another country with four young children, leaving behind everyone they knew, all in order to access the opportunities that Fiji could not provide.

Today, when I think back to those early swimming lessons under the watchful gaze of my mother, I remember the second pool in the complex, separated from the main pool by a small walkway. In that pool was my father. Like me, he was splashing and blowing bubbles as he, too, learned how to float in a mirror of my own lessons. A lone adult, being taught by someone a decade younger than him, was learning a skill that almost every other adult in the place had acquired as a child.

But my father didn't have the insecurities of his child. He felt no shame about being a beginner, at not knowing something, understanding as he did that it was a difference of circumstance, not a difference of ability that put him in the water instead of on the sidelines. He felt only excitement at learning something new, and determination to gain the skills he needed to protect his children in this new, Australian life.

When I think about this now, I am in awe of his confidence, his certainty. I can't think of a single time in those early years in Albury when my father seemed embarrassed or discomfited by his cultural difference. He was the man who would take his daughters to the roller-skating park at six in the morning so they could practise before the 'hooligans' (his word, not mine) arrived. He was the man who would chat to a stranger at the grocery store and end up going to their house for a coffee, always learning more about our fellow Australians. At a time before many Australians understood what halal meant to Muslims, he brokered connections with local farmers so he could purchase and slaughter animals on their property in order to provide his family with halal meat.

My insecurities were not inherited from my parents. They are, however, a legacy shared with many other young people who grew up as first-generation migrants. When I reflect on my parents' journey and sacrifice, my choice not to engage in the very activities that they fought to win for us, out of fear or embarrassment, feels wrong. How dare I avoid the pool or beach when my parents had to swim against so many tides to bring us here, to a country where I can walk across the road from my apartment to a clean pool?

I doubt I will ever feel entirely at ease in water. My swimming is ungainly, and I tire quickly. My body is more comfortable on land than in the ocean. But I feel a duty to enjoy the privileges of my citizenship – the access to leisure facilities and medical aid for my arthritis are both things that I may have had to live without in Fiji, unless my parents were able to carve out an equally successful life there as they have here.

So I force myself back to the pool, week after week. I ignore the thudding of my heart and slip into the water, striking out with a confidence I don't feel. And when I go back outside, under the crisp, blue Canberra sky, I whisper a thanks to my parents for their strength in coming here. What they have given me, I won't forsake so easily.

BIDDING THE *BIDAAI* – MARRIAGE, FAREWELLS AND FEMINISM

It was a scorching summer the year my eldest sister, Zaheeda, got married. Fijian summers are always pretty shocking, but I remember December 2004 as being particularly hideous. The wind barely rippled the grass or the heavy-hanging trees outside our hotel room windows, the humidity weighing them down, keeping them sodden and still. Within minutes of leaving the hotel, our clothes were covered in sweat patches, and showers offered only a brief respite. I couldn't think of a less romantic climate for a wedding.

Zaheeda was excited about her impending marriage to Afraaz, but I found it hard to hide my melancholy. Zaheeda was my favourite person in the world. She was my mentor, my best friend and, when I was younger, a sort of second mother figure. I hated that she was starting this new chapter that would take her away from us. My other sister, Zakia, was also a central part of my life, but being closer in age our relationship was more that of equals, whereas Zaheeda – although only three years older than me – already seemed like a sophisticated woman.

In the week before the wedding I lay around our hotel room in a malaise, trying to hold onto every minute that Zaheeda was still part of our family and not yet given over to her husband's. Eventually the wedding day was upon us. The humidity was as draining as ever, the air itself ensnaring us and making every minute drag. We sat in the segregated hall of the local high school that was doubling as the wedding venue, passing tin kettles of ice-cold Tang and plastic cups along the rows of women in an effort to keep our guests from dehydrating. Zakia sat beside Zaheeda at the front of the room, while as the youngest sister I sat with my mother and aunts. We were all dressed in stunning traditional clothes, but Zaheeda's two-toned blue *ghagra choli* was exquisite. She made a beautiful bride. Although I felt awkward wearing Indian clothes in Australia, in Fiji it felt natural, surrounded as we were by so many other Fijian-Indians dressed in traditional outfits. Zakia and I had matching pink bridesmaids' *kameez*es, and I felt beautiful in mine.

After the ceremony (which seemed to go on forever, my teenage brain remembers), we all moved to several classrooms attached to the hall and sat at the high school–sized desks to eat home-cooked curry and roti doled out by relatives. And then it was time for the *bidaai*.

Bidaai in Hindi means 'to bid farewell'. In a wedding context, it is the moment when the bride's family formally farewells her and passes her to her husband's family. The ritual takes different forms according to the religious traditions of the wedding, but at the ceremonies I have attended it consists of the bride hugging and taking blessings from her relatives in order from the eldest down, and with her immediate family taking precedence. This, to me, has always been the most stressful part of a wedding. It is emotionally overwrought, but also deeply ceremonial. Physical displays of emotion aren't common in my family. We show our love for each other through our actions (like my mother's cooking). To see so many of my relatives crying openly during the *bidaai* always felt strange to me.

At other family weddings I was usually distracted by worrying about doing the wrong thing during the ritual, but this time there was no avoiding the emotion. I watched, my heart thumping, as my mother and father hugged Zaheeda, tears in their eyes, while her new husband, Afraaz, stood respectfully beside her. My brother gruffly joined them, and then Zakia hugged Zaheeda tightly, managing to give herself a blood nose, which introduced a welcome moment of levity. For a few minutes, the procession was halted while aunties rummaged in their bags for tissues, and Zakia pinched her nose and leaned back. Zaheeda laughed through her tears and checked her dress for stains, and it was as though we all gave a collective breath out before the *bidaai* started again.

I hung back and watched them moving along the line. For a moment I thought I would be forgotten, but hands pressed into my back and I was pushed forward through the crowd, hugging my sister and feeling her pull away from me.

It was a big moment, the heat making sweat linger in the creases of our elbows, mingling with tears in the corners of our eyes. My clothes were hot and itchy, and I felt drained by the weight of strangers' eyes on my face. The hug felt unreal. It was meant to be meaningful, but I kept thinking of the times we had hugged in laughter at home while watching *The Princess Bride*, and all the hugs I gave Zaheeda when I visited her that year while she was living away at university. She was the first of the family to live outside of home, sanctioned by my parents because there was no way for her to study pharmacy in Canberra. I had missed her so much when she left – I wrote her letters and made her mix CDs, unable to come to terms with the hole she left in my life. This hug was for show, but it was also our last before she was taken even further from me – or at least that was what I feared at the time.

When we finally left, the decorations pulled down and the cars loaded with empty pots and pans from lunch, I felt hollow. The hotel room felt dim without Zaheeda's brightness, and our family seemed to have shrunk, reconfigured from our tight-knit unit of six to something different.

The next day we went to my new brother-in-law's parents' house for the *walimah* (wedding reception), traditionally hosted by the groom's family. There was Zaheeda, in clothes picked out by her in-laws. She already seemed far away from me, from our shared history. She was a grown woman now, with her own family, made up of her and Afraaz.

Of course, once the commotion of the wedding had subsided, my fears about the *bidaai* keeping us from each other turned out to be unfounded. Zaheeda and Afraaz flew to Australia a few weeks after us, and in the more than a decade since they have remained firmly part of our family, regardless of the cultural rules that say she should be closer to her husband's people than her own. Their distance is built from actual miles – Afraaz's family is now in New Zealand, physically separate though still a big part of their lives.

In the intervening years, I have come to see the *bidaai* for what it is – the sealing of a contract, historically made between men, passing the 'burden' of a woman from one to another. Its origins are sexist, even if it isn't meant that way today. And like many aspects of my Indian heritage, large and small, it bothers me, even if it doesn't bother anyone else I know.

It's important to point out here that the term 'Indian culture' is broad enough to be essentially meaningless. As I've mentioned before, there is no one Indian culture – the states are divided from each other by different traditions and languages, and through the extraordinarily wideranging Indian diaspora, traditions have become twisted and transformed over generations. Religion also plays its part. So, to be fair, I should say that what troubled me was possibly specific to Indo-Fijian-Muslim-Gujarati culture as I have witnessed it in my life.

Many of the things that niggled at me were small and ordinary, often absorbed into the normalcy of our day-to-day lives. The *bidaai* encapsulated a lot of the smaller customs that, to me, mark the significant influence of patriarchy in the enactment of family and community relationships in our culture. In its traditional sense, the *bidaai* means that a woman is no longer the responsibility of her own parents and is now subject to the command of her husband and his family. It's easy to see how this framing of marriage is problematic. For many women, the consequences are horrific. Even today, there are documented cases of women being forced to live in conditions of near slavery in their in-laws' homes. In some cases, women have suffered physical and emotional abuse that has been likened to torture, perpetrated by the parents-in-law as well as the husband.

This abuse is part of an institutionalised patriarchal system in India that sees women as chattels, and enables older women to inflict the same abuse they once suffered onto the younger women entering their homes. It is a system that is outdated, and in many parts of India entirely ignored – but it persists elsewhere, especially in poorer and rural areas. Unfortunately, it has also travelled with Indian communities into the diaspora.

Another component of this issue is the system of dowries – payment made by a bride's family to her husband as compensation for taking on the 'burden' of their daughter. Although dowries are now technically illegal in India, the practice continues, and it can lead to extortion of a bride's family, as well as abuse inflicted on the woman as punishment for a dowry considered insufficient. In some cases, even after a dowry amount is agreed between two families, the groom will demand additional payment from his in-laws, using his wife's safety and the stability of the marriage as leverage. If a woman were to be divorced after the marriage is consummated, this could have devastating effects on her reputation and ability to remarry, so the threat is very real.

The dowry system persists among Indian communities in Australia as well. This issue has been targeted by women such as Dr Manjula O'Connor, who has for years led a campaign to criminalise dowries in Australia. But how do you police something that happens largely behind closed doors, and which is so tied up in notions of honour and reputation? Dr O'Connor has spoken publicly about the aggression she has faced from the Australian-Indian community in response to her activism, which is seen as a threat to their way of life. And in times of intense political correctness, where any critique of cultural traditions can be viewed as prejudiced, it's even harder to protest against an issue so complex without being seen as infringing the rights of migrant communities to retain their culture in the diaspora.

I am lucky to have grown up in a family that doesn't condone or support dowries, or the patriarchal approach to marriage that sees women as possessions. My parents have always been fiercely determined that their daughters will be highly educated and will exercise choice in who they marry.

Crucially, if I make decisions that step outside the bounds of what my parents approve of, the consequences are only emotional – I never have to fear of physical retribution. This is not the case for many Indian women, both in India and in the diaspora. Physical punishment, including acid attacks and other forms of assault, play a significant part in the marriage culture of India and are linked to the persistent notion of women as property within the patriarchal system of family relationships. Parents may choose to punish their daughters to dissuade them from dishonouring the family name by engaging in relationships outside of marriage, or from refusing a match that is proposed to them. This occurs both in India and in migrant communities across the world.

In 2003, English teenager Shafilea Ahmed was murdered by her parents for wanting to live a 'western lifestyle' and refusing to enter an arranged marriage. Farzana and Iftikhar Ahmed colluded in suffocating their daughter in front of their other children, and her father later dumped her body in a river. When I heard about this case, I was dumbstruck. This girl was just a few years older than me. I, too, was torn between a western culture and Islam. I, too, had parents who would prefer me to have an arranged marriage and to remain a devout Muslim. But my parents believe in choice and individual autonomy. That doesn't mean they condone all of my decisions, but they accept that they can't control their children's every choice. Shafilea was not so lucky, and her murder suggests that her parents saw her as both their property and their burden to dispose of.

When I think about the *bidaai* in the context of this broader pattern of patriarchal control, the symbolism is sinister. The bride is not just bidding farewell to her family and her old life, she is bidding farewell to her selfhood and her identity pre-wedding. Every day I am grateful that I was born into a family that is loving, and fair, and that has spent years working through our differences as people together. But I fear for other young women of the diaspora like Shafilea, growing up caught between two cultures, within families and communities far less forgiving.

I grew up in the 1990s and early 2000s, at a time when feminism was distinctly unfashionable. There was a strong sense among students at my school that gender inequality was not something our generation needed to worry about. It certainly wasn't a topic most of my friends wanted to discuss. I was just getting involved with *Lip*, and my interest in feminism was growing. I was reading Simone de Beauvoir and Naomi Wolf, and had many 'aha!' moments as I saw their critiques of gender norms playing out around me. But the general consensus among my peers was that gender equality already existed, and that feminists were taking things too far, focusing on the negatives and not the positives.

I can see how a white teenager growing up in Canberra in that era might have felt like this. In all the ways that mattered at that age, men and women were indeed equal. Or rather, cisgender heterosexual men and women were equal(ish). Women nominally had equal pay (though we know that access to the workforce and to leadership roles mean that there is a considerable gap between women's and men's take-home pay), enrolment rates for women in tertiary institutes were higher than those of men, and as teenagers we didn't yet see how gender stereotypes in the workforce or the lack of paid parental leave would affect us. Gender inequality is largely invisible to teens, because the impacts are only felt when women enter the workforce and feel the true outcomes of the gender pay gap and the unconscious bias that prevents women from rising through the ranks in many industries.

As a result, feminism often became relevant for middle-class teenagers only when they also identified with one or more minority groups. It was intersectionality in action – for teenagers in minority groups (whether relating to race, sexuality, ability or body shape), gender inequality intersected with the barriers we faced as a result of our other differences. Looking back, the true heroes of our school were the young women who didn't conform to conventional beauty standards, and/or who were open in their bisexuality or queer identities. They had to publicly account for themselves in the face of daily rejection and ridicule from their peers. I never witnessed public shaming of overweight boys in our school as I did of girls, who were taunted for not conforming to the two options available to young women – either to meet conventional standards of physical attractiveness or to be invisible.

I was intrigued by a lesbian couple in my sister's year, who were forced to exist on the fringes of their year group's social life. Zakia, who was good friends with them, was one of the few teenagers in the school who hung out with these girls and demonstrated how little their sexuality was any of her business. I remember looking at the couple as they walked the perimeter of the school oval at lunchtime, cigarettes in hand, and thinking that it must have been tough not to conform. But another part of me wondered why two pretty white girls wouldn't just hide their difference and fit in. They *could* hide their sexuality, my little teenage brain thought. I couldn't hide my brownness, but if I could have walked out of school and found an all-white skin concealer, I probably would have. So why didn't they take the 'easy' option available to them? I realise now that my experience of race and their experience of sexuality were more similar than I appreciated at the time. These are two inherent facets of our identity that we cannot change (and why should we want to?).

While I did experience racial prejudice, I didn't face obvious gender-based discrimination at school. However, I did see the gender gap quite clearly in traditional practices at home, and it grated on me. It was little things. In the ways that mattered, my immediate family was far more progressive than our extended family. My parents were as proud of and ambitious for their daughters as for their son, and they modelled gender equality in the way they ran our family – both of them worked hard, and both of them had a say in our finances and the way their children were raised. Yet there were still aspects of our lives that frustrated me. For example, the fact that at social gatherings women were in charge of cooking, making tea and serving the men, who sat and received their victuals and left their dirty dishes for us to clean up later. Or how the local mosque in Canberra at the time had two huge spaces where men could pray, while women were relegated to a small balcony a quarter of the size. During Eid, the women would often end up on the grass outside the mosque. Arguably, there were more men than women who came to pray. But conversely, the lack of space acted as a deterrent – the experience each year of being crammed in so close to the other women that I could barely bend and had to put my face uncomfortably close to the butt of the woman in front of me every time I kneeled forward in prayer made me determined to get permission to pray at home the following Eid.

There was also the way that Islam and, in a different way, broader Indian culture policed women's clothing while largely letting men do whatever they wanted. I'm pretty sure that if my brother had come home with his hair in a mohawk and wearing a singlet and tight shorts my parents would have had something to say about it (as would most mainstream, semi-conservative white parents), but the restrictions on women's clothing were far more detailed and extended to condemning practices that are very normalised in a western context (like wearing close-fitting jeans or skirts above calf length, or, in more extreme cases, wearing any visible makeup). These restrictions were also openly enforced through gossiping and staring at public gatherings.

These things can seem largely innocuous in themselves, and (particularly in relation to clothing) are often driven by aspects of personal faith that perhaps aren't for me to criticise. Further, I can see that even in my own lifetime there has been swift progress in addressing gender inequality within the diasporic Indian culture I grew up with. But when viewed through the lens of history, and the legacy of monstrous violence enacted against Indian women by the patriarchal culture of the country, these remnants of defined gender roles set my nerves on edge.

When you think about traditions such as bride burning in Hindu culture, dowries and child marriages, or the high rates of female infant mortality, the nuggets of gender inequality that persist in modern Indian culture as practised in the diaspora become more problematic. They belong to a belief system that sees women as inferior, and as largely powerless in their communities.

Importantly, rigid gender roles in any culture have a negative impact on both men and women (and an even stronger negative impact on those who don't identify with a binary gender or the gender they were assigned at birth). As little as I enjoyed being on kitchen duty or having to serve our male guests their tea at gatherings, I was also glad that I didn't have to help my dad butcher chickens in the backyard, or retile an entire bathroom, like my brother did. Now, my brother absolutely loves to cook, something I never would have guessed because he was never encouraged to try it as a young man, instead being expected to stick to the masculine tasks assigned to him. As a fifteen-year-old, my analysis of the situation at hand was not sophisticated enough for me to see how men also suffered from the expectations around gender norms. And the fact remains that although men might have yearned for access to traditionally feminine activities, the judgement cast on them was less intense than that on women, who were always aware of the watchful gaze of society.

It's the notion of these unseen eyes that has always fuelled my determination as a feminist. It's the policing of our bodies that is so ubiquitous that we internalise it and shame ourselves into dressing in certain ways. It's the raised eyebrows that remind us that our physical modesty does not reflect only on ourselves but also on our families and the way our parents raised us.

And while some of this is specific to Indian culture, versions of this body-shaming and reinforcement of gender norms certainly exist in Australia as well, creating a dual barrier for many migrant women who are forced to live between both sets of expectations.

I've always felt conflicted about talking about the issue of gender inequality in Indian culture because I feel defensive of my heritage, and also because I don't want people to assume that my criticism of it implies a contrastingly favourable view of Australian culture. Modern western societies like to give themselves a big pat on the back for supposedly being so much more progressive and equal than developing countries. Women in the west are certainly less visibly confined by gender norms, but the patriarchy is insidious, and it's usually what you can't see that you should be paying attention to.

In 2012, when a young woman was brutally and fatally gang-raped in Delhi, India, the west jumped to condemn India's 'rape problem'. Several countries issued travel warnings for women intending to travel to India, and a professor from Leipzig University in Germany barred a male Indian student from an internship due to India's 'rape problem'. These reactions were toxic and patronising. In fact, as contributing editor of the *Berkley Political Review* Bhaavya Sinha points out in her article 'The Adverse Effects of the Western Fixation on India's "Rape Problem"', when western countries are quick to point the finger at developing countries with 'gender problems', this attitude only reinforces the west's problematic self-positioning as culturally superior to the developing world. In India's case in particular, this is deeply troubling, given that the country is still recovering from the long-lasting effects of British colonialism.[12]

It is also far-fetched to suggest that the west has solved the issue of violence against women. One in four women in Australia has experienced at least one instance of male-perpetrated violence. And there is overwhelming evidence that victims of sexual assault in western, first-world countries are as unlikely as their Indian counterparts to be believed and to see the perpetrators held to account. Gender equality shouldn't be seen as some sort of global pissing contest. Yet, in my experience, many white Australians have a smug attitude when it comes to people of colour, assuming that we are somehow less advanced and liberated than they are.

Some years ago, my father attended a parent–teacher interview at high school with my sister Zakia, when she had a minor problem with an assessment piece in history. When the teacher told Dad about the problem, he turned to Zakia and said in a jokingly menacing tone, 'Well, we'll be having a talk about this at home, won't we?', at which she rolled her eyes.

The following day, the teacher took me aside to ask me if everything was okay at home. She took her time impressing on me that if my father was ever violent, I could tell her. I was mortified. My father has never been violent. When we were little and did something naughty, he used to do a fake slap, where he put his hand against us and clapped it with his other hand, making a loud noise but usually just making us burst into fits of giggles. To assume, based on nothing more than a single comment at a parent-teacher interview, that we were abused and needed a white saviour to step in is such a banally racist response, it still makes me flush with anger. It plays into the notion that non-western cultures are inherently barbaric, or not held to the rules of polite society as Australian culture supposedly is.

As a teenager flying the feminist flag, I hadn't yet fully grasped the whiteness of feminism – that the ideologies of liberal feminism, taught to me by writers such as Germaine Greer and Ariel Levy, are constructed with an almost entirely white audience in mind.

These ideologies are very straightforward – women should have the choice to decide how they want to live their lives, free from gender norms. Women should be safe, free, able to do whatever they want with their bodies. The way to address gender norms is through cultural change. And once the culture is changed, all women will have equal access to the opportunities that have been denied to them.

By using the label 'women', liberal feminism dug its own grave. 'Women' is a broad term. It could be construed as being an inclusive term, but it is in fact an essentialising term that allows the white mainstream to bypass minority issues in favour of the majority. The use of 'women' in a lot of mainstream feminist rhetoric implied that the norm for all women is to be white, to be middle-class and to have access to education. But we know that all women are not made equal. Issues of class, race, ability, mental health and sexuality are intrinsically linked to gender identity, and greatly affect an individual's ability to access the life they want, and to live free from prejudice. If liberal feminists wanted to be more representative and accurate in their use of the term 'women', they would have to lobby for issues primarily affecting minority cultures with the same zeal they have applied to the broader issues they target – and this would inevitably mean widening the discussion from gender equality to racial equality, and economic equality.

It seems odd today, in a time when intersectionality is becoming widely understood, to imagine a feminism that is primarily occupied with issues affecting straight, middle-class white women. I spent years working for a feminist not-for-profit, and saw how conscious the organisation was of the need to address diversity in our campaigns and events, and to make sure that minority voices were being heard. This type of active inclusion was the result of years of women in marginalised groups being outspoken and unflinching in their criticism of the status quo – from the African-American poet and activist Audre Lorde speaking out for black women in the 1960s and 1970s, through to women like the late Stella Young in Australia fighting for the rights of women living with disability over the past decade. The days of Sheryl Sandberg's capitalist, white, liberal approach in *Lean In* seem mostly behind us, but in a way the damage is already done, because there remain some stereotypes of women of colour that are hard to shake. One is the trope of the meek, submissive Muslim woman. And one of the effects of these stereotypes is that when women of colour want to call out an issue of gender inequality within our culture, it feels as though we're somehow feeding into the false assumptions about the barbaric norms that supposedly subjugate all of us as one faceless group.

When explaining my cultural heritage to a stranger, I have learned to expect a certain response. As a teenager, I felt quite judged for being Muslim, both because of a generalised sense of Islamophobia post–September 11, but also because there was an underlying assumption that my parents (especially my father) were strict and unforgiving, maybe even abusive. My parents *were* protective by western standards, but they were far from the stern jailkeepers well-meaning westerners wanted to assume. My father is a quick-witted, compassionate, progressive and driven by his values, many of which (like charity and cultural equality) are reinforced by his religion. He is not a cookie-cutter patriarch I need saving from. Equally importantly, my mother is a strong, intelligent, brave and capable woman who has never been a shrinking violet. She can hold her own in any argument, and would probably laugh out loud at the idea of being labelled meek or submissive when it comes to her relationship with her husband. They are a team. They are not a microcosm of the patriarchy that exists within the broadest possible definition of Islam.

This anxiety at the thought of my family being stereotyped inhibited me from really interrogating and picking apart the aspects of our culture that did bother me, and that I felt were infringing on my identity as a woman. How could I complain about something as minor as the cultural expectations of dressing in a certain way to be seen as 'modest', when in doing so I might confirm the negative view most people already had of Islam as a controlling, patriarchal religion?

Because mainstream feminism has made little attempt to engage with women of colour about these issues, I also felt a lot of responsibility to ensure my views were broadly applicable and relevant to as many different kinds of Muslim women as I could. I knew that this was effectively impossible, but I also knew that mainstream feminism would assume that one Muslim woman's experience was indicative of that of every Muslim woman, and I wanted to avoid doing our community damage.

Eventually, when I stopped practising Islam at eighteen, I felt largely set free from this anxiety. 'See,' I could say, 'I'm an infidel. What do I know about Islam? I don't speak for Muslim women.' It was liberating. I still felt protective of the religion I was raised with and that my parents practise, but I didn't have to feel like an unwilling ambassador.

Even so, the feminist sources I tried to turn to for help were largely whitewashed. I could not find any easily accessible Australian resource, whether pop culture, a book or an online article, that spoke about feminism in a way that wasn't automatically targeted at middle-class white women. *Lip* was the closest thing I found, but content that actively took a diverse perspective was pretty thin on the ground. Of course, the sources I looked to were largely created *by* white women, and as a result had a tone and message that were also *for* them. But it was also a sign of the times, in that some of the key issues that liberal feminism was interrogating when I was a teenager were just so far removed from my Muslim upbringing that I couldn't relate at all.

The concept of raunch feminism, for example, felt entirely alien. I read Ariel Levy's 2005 book *Female Chauvinist Pigs* and felt somewhat gratified that Levy saw problematic aspects to raunch feminism as well. The basic premise of raunch feminism is that women should exercise freedom of choice in regard to their bodies, and that previous feminist campaigns that protested against the sexualisation of female bodies denied women the right to be empowered by their sexuality. This is a really brief summary, but the idea that our bodies were ours to flaunt was a little hard for me to connect with, given that I was still trying to determine whether my body was mine to dress in jeans and a normal t-shirt that didn't entirely cover my bum. Raunch culture was so far removed from my experience as a young Muslim, and most feminist channels at the time (magazines and books, in the pre-internet phase of my life) were so saturated in it, that I felt myself to be on the fringes of feminism.

And when mainstream feminists did take it upon themselves to publicly show concern over a minority issue, they usually made blanket statements that ignored the complexity of the matter. Take, for example, the issue of hijabs and burqas worn by Muslim women. The burqa is a long head covering that generally leaves the face visible but covers the woman's torso, whereas the hijab is a shorter covering of just the hair.

People often confuse the burqa with the niqab, which also covers the woman's face, leaving a slit for her eyes only. In the 2000s, many white feminists were in favour of banning the burqa, because it was supposedly a patriarchal tool used by Muslim men to control their wives and daughters. Well-known feminists protested against the garment, without seeming to understand that Muslim women are individuals first, Muslims second. Yes, undoubtedly the burqa is used to control women in some contexts. But equally, wearing it is a choice for many women, some of my relatives included. Most importantly, it is not up to white feminists to 'save' Muslim women from aspects of their religion, especially without including them in the conversation.

By contrast, feminism today is so concerned with not appearing racist or Islamophobic that the loudest and highest-profile voices support the hijab (or are silent on it), to the point where Muslim women who don't wear the hijab feel ignored and abandoned by the movement. In 2013, white women were encouraged to wear a hijab for 'World Hijab Day', a campaign founded by a young Muslim woman. The internet was flooded with selfies of white women donning hijabs and grinning. In response, two Muslim women, Asra Q Nomani and Hala Arafa, wrote an article pointing out that they, and many other women, did not see the hijab as representative of their faith. Their argument was largely ignored, because mainstream feminism lacks the complexity that would enable it to reconcile two different opinions held by Muslim women.

Because of this lack of engagement with the relevant communities, and the inability to see individual cultural groups as multifaceted and diverse (that's right, not all Muslim women are the same), feminism creates conversations that shut out groups of women at each turn. Perhaps the issue is that liberal feminism focuses so much on identity and using our personal communication channels to show support for an issue that it's easier for the women to just wear the hijab and take a selfie to show that they generally support Muslim women and religious diversity than it would be to find a more meaningful way to connect with the issue, one that might require more research and groundwork with the communities at hand.

In addition, most mainstream feminism these days is largely focused on effecting 'cultural change' without following this up with the policies required to facilitate said change. If we take the debate about the burqa as an example, it's clear that the real issue here is domestic violence. Those who argue against the burqa are concerned that Muslim women could be suffering from abuse at the hands of their husbands, and they see the goal as being to free women to choose what they wear, based on their erroneous assumption that the burqa can only be a tool of control.

No one in my family has ever worn the burqa other than when actually praying, but my mother wears the hijab proudly. When the 'ban the burqa' debate (the first round anyway) was at its height in the late 2000s, I was a uni student. I felt furious whenever the discussion implied that women like my mother were exercising anything less than their personal choice when expressing their faith through the hijab. It was equally offensive to think that people assumed my dad was forcing her to do so, and that he held such regressive views about women and their rights and freedoms.

If you're concerned about domestic violence in minority communities, why not consult with those communities and work together to lobby for more effective reporting and sentencing processes, which would make it easier for women to report abuse if they experience it, and deter men from inflicting abuse through the threat of harsh punishments? Why not lobby for primary prevention education programs for young men, regardless of ethnicity, to ensure that gender equality is a value that is instilled in men from a young age, which might prevent instances of abuse in the future? Why not call for greater funding and access to translation services for women so that they can report abuse in their own language and aren't hindered by a language barrier? Why jump straight to banning the burqa, an outcome that would only cause significant loss of identity for Muslim women, and potentially result in some women no longer entering the public sphere because they aren't appropriately dressed, according to their religious beliefs?

The ban the burqa debate is a perfect example of liberal feminism taking a top-down approach to gender equality in diverse communities, one that is more about white feminists posturing in public than it is about creating lasting change.

In the years after Zaheeda's wedding, her *bidaai* became a distant memory. She and Afraaz have built a rich life together, which now includes three of the loveliest, smartest little girls in the world. Our family is closer than ever.

I enjoy the symbolic aspects of our culture. I enjoy the way we mark momentous occasions and take time to acknowledge the way our families grow and change, and how our identities transform with each new milestone.

It's true that each marriage marks an end to a chapter in our family's life, just as each birth and addition starts a new one. Since Zaheeda's wedding – the first big change – we have welcomed another spouse and five children into our family, and our gatherings have become immense. In that hotel room in Fiji, I was right to mourn the loss of our old family life. Gone were the days of the six of us living in a bubble of our own. But I wish I had known to look forward to the changes instead of dreading them, because our lives and relationships are definitely richer for them.

When I look at my four nieces and my nephew, I wonder how different their experiences of our Indian culture will be from my own. Each generation changes, and every year society moves us in a slightly different direction. As parents, my siblings have their own unique ways of engaging their kids with our cultural heritage. I watch my eldest niece, Umaiza, and how much she loves her Indian clothes and having henna painted onto her hands at Eid. I enjoy her exuberance, and her joy in these traditions. I see how little the gender-coded norms of our culture affect her life so far, and I wonder if they will begin to be more apparent as she gets older.

Feminism is an ever-changing beast, and the current focus on intersectionality is a move in the right direction. But I hope that my nieces and nephew have access to a world that celebrates difference while acknowledging that no one identity marker can truly define a person, and that gender should only ever form part of the picture.

HOW TO BE AN ALLY TO PEOPLE OF COLOUR – TAKE TWO

The anecdote I'm about to share is a fairly innocuous one, on the surface. It is not the type of interaction that most white people would consider to be the most grievous or damaging example of racism. It's definitely not the worst experience of racism I've ever had, either. But it has stuck with me in a way that many more shocking incidents haven't. Where they have blurred and faded as time passes, probably as part of a self-protection mechanism, this story has only become clearer as a focal point for my anger.

In 2013 I was working for an industry peak body in Barton, the Canberra suburb where many public service departments and lobbying organisations are located. Barton is Canberra in a nutshell – a leafy suburb with wide avenues, where every person you see is wearing a lanyard and holding a latte, the epitome of all the stereotypes about soulless public servants that Canberra-bashing is built on. I was 23, in just my second professional role, and I still felt very much as though I was play-acting my way through life. Every day at work I had the curious sensation that I was completely making it up – what did I know about writing media releases or taking meeting minutes?

That day, I was sick. Miserable, runny-nosed, can't-get-out-of-bed sick, but I had dragged myself in to work anyway. At lunchtime, I walked to the Rugby Union Club next door to our building (the nearest place that sold food) and waited in a massive line. When I arrived at the counter, I ordered a sandwich (the only vegetarian option on the menu), only to be told in a sullen tone by the burly man on the cash register that they didn't sell sandwiches after midday. Given that sandwiches are a classic lunch food, this was confusing to me, so I frowned, and then said it was okay and turned to leave.

At this point, he leaned forward and jeered, 'Wait, don't go – we can make you a nice curry!' and then he and most of the line behind me chuckled.

I walked as quickly as I could out of the club, my heart hammering, and went back to my desk without buying any food. I left work early that day, and couldn't stop replaying the scene in my head. It was the sort of casual, public racism that I hadn't experienced in a long time. Not since high school had I been derided in public, or clearly made to feel part of an out-group. The racism I had experienced most often was more insidious, subtle, like muttered comments in a restaurant, or people addressing me with a certain look or tone of voice. This was blatant, and humiliating in how visible it was. At home, I told Chris about the incident, and he was angry, although nowhere near as upset as I was. At the time, I put this down to the facts that he wasn't there himself and wasn't the target of the racism.

When I visited my parents' house for dinner that week, I relayed the story to them and my sister. Their response was unexpected – instead of simply being angry at the man behind the counter, they were also disappointed in me. 'Why didn't you say something to him?' Dad asked. 'We didn't raise you to run away.'

I was annoyed by this (was I to be a victim of casual racism *and* have the blame laid at my feet?), but I can now see where they were coming from. To my family, racism was an ugly reality, a given in our daily lives, something that was impossible to avoid. We cannot control who is racist to us, all we can control is our response, and my father wanted me to respond with pride and dignity, not by scurrying away.

So why didn't I say something? Why didn't I give the man a cold stare, and say, 'Excuse me, but I'm not sure what you're implying with that comment. Would you care to explain?' Why did I flush, and walk stiffly away, my heart pounding and my palms sweaty? It's a simple answer, but one that has taken me many hours of ruminating to realise. I didn't say anything because I didn't feel entirely confident that I *was* being subjected to racism.

My immediate response when confronted with racism in an ordinary interaction, like being served in a cafe or at the supermarket, or when someone yells out a car window some casual slur ('Go home' or 'Love it or leave it', et cetera), is to assume that I misheard them, or second-guess whether they were directing their hate at me. This is a sort of gaslighting that occurs with racism, where POC can never be entirely sure that we're not overreacting, or that we're not just looking for ways to reinforce our victim status.

Perhaps, I have told myself, the man in the club was genuinely offering me an alternative lunch. Perhaps curry was in fact the special that day. Perhaps I imagined the jeering tone in his voice, or the malicious glint in his eye. It is so easy to excuse or explain away racism as a misunderstanding between two individuals, a case of he said, she said.

I have no doubt that by leaving I reinforced his sense of power in that interaction. But I'm not convinced that my saying something would have done anything to redress the balance. It might have actually placed me in a more vulnerable position, especially as a woman and as a young person, surrounded by strangers. In any case, the fact is that I didn't stand up to my demons, and I have rarely done so in my life so far. Most often, I burn with shame and anger, and keep my jaw stiff and eyes downcast as I try to leave the ugliness of the interaction behind me.

My family's reaction to the incident reminded me that the responsibility to address prejudice and discrimination in Australia generally falls on the marginalised party. The onus is always on us to report incidents, to call out transgressions, to make our voices louder than those of our detractors. My father wanted me to stand up to that man because he knows that there is no other recourse for a POC than to take justice into their own hands, and to rely on their own voice.

But why should this be the case? I live in a majority white city, in a country founded on the legacy of white supremacy, and I know that the white people who form my primary social group all consider themselves to be allies to POC. And yet, when I experience racism and tell my friends about it, they often suggest that I have misinterpreted the incident. In high school, references to racism were regularly met with disbelief – my peers would say things to the effect of 'Racism doesn't happen here' or 'I've never seen anyone being racist in this city'. 'Of course you haven't,' I wanted to scream. 'You're white, and I'm the only POC you spend any time with!'

I know that white people's denial of the reality of racism is most often born of a refusal to believe that progress hasn't been made, and disbelief that people can still be prejudiced in the cities and country they love. In her book *Why I'm No Longer Talking to White People About Race*, British journalist Reni Eddo-Lodge uses the term 'Nice White People' to describe this kind of reaction from progressive, well-meaning white people who, in an attempt to deal with their own anxiety and guilt at being part of the perpetrating group, deny the experiences of POC and ultimately deny the existence of racism.[13]

But POC don't have that privilege. We have no choice but to confront the ugliest aspects of the culture we love, because we are the direct targets of the hate. And when we're personally affected by racism, disbelief and denial are the least helpful responses we can receive from our white communities.

In 2015, I wrote an article for *Right Now* magazine titled 'How to Be an Ally to People of Colour'. I wrote it in a flurry after a frustrating week when I felt my experience had been denied or troubled by Chris. Unintentionally, he had responded to an incident when I felt I had been treated with hostility because of my race by denying my experience and putting the blame at my feet. He said it didn't sound as though I had experienced racism, and maybe I was being sensitive about the incident. I was furious and upset. It was hurtful to have my experience diminished and then to be held responsible for how I 'interpreted' someone else's negative behaviour.

As I told him later, regardless of whether the individual experience was motivated by racism, the fact that I have experienced so much direct racism during my life in Australia means that every new interaction with white people that is even slightly negative carries the baggage of 24 years of shame and othering. Whether or not each moment can be conclusively proven to be an incidence of racism is irrelevant – my emotional response cannot be rational, and it also can't be 'wrong', because it is a result of ingrained marginalisation that has followed me and my ancestors through centuries of postcolonial displacement and disadvantage. This is not to say that POC can never be wrong in their response to racism – violence is wrong, under any circumstances, and the intention of the people involved needs to be understood in order to work through any conflict. But assessing something as racist or not is as much about how it makes the victim feel as it is about how the perpetrator intended their action.

As I wrote the article, I found myself sifting back through the many times that I had experienced discrimination and chosen not to tell my non-POC friends or networks about it. It occurred to me that I often didn't relay these incidents because I was ashamed – and that lurking under that shame was a fear that I would be considered weak or melodramatic for holding onto these fleeting moments of hate. I didn't want to be disbelieved – and yet that is the response I most often received when I did open up about my experiences. Even writing this now, I am worried that my friends will see me as self-victimising, overreacting and creating a mountain out of a molehill.

White people's desire to challenge individual experiences of racism told to them by POC often comes from a desire to challenge the existence of racism itself. When Chris suggests that I have mistaken someone's behaviour for racism, what he is subconsciously asserting is his own disbelief that racism could exist, and his unwillingness to accept that the country that he loves could produce such hate. He is becoming a 'Nice White Person', despite his good intentions.

When I do tell my friends about racism I have experienced, it is driven by two impulses. First, to expel the experience from my body – to let it out, in the hopes that the sensations of fear, anger and despair that it conjured in me can also be expelled. And second, I am seeking validation that my experience warranted those emotions, and that the perpetrator of racism is irrevocably wrong. I want to see that wrongness on my friends' faces when they listen to my retelling. I want their sympathy and acknowledgment to hold that wrongness in front of me, as proof that racism is unfounded and that the crime lies at the feet of the perpetrator, and not at mine. Yet I rarely receive this validation.

My experience is in no way isolated. As Eddo-Lodge writes of white reactions to stories of racial prejudice, 'They've never had to think about what it means, in power terms, to be white, so any time they're vaguely reminded of this fact, they interpret it as an affront.'[14] Eddo-Lodge goes on to describe the way that POC are often expected to prioritise 'white feelings' when trying to work towards a combined understanding of racism. We have to make white people feel better about the racism their peers commit.

In the years since I wrote the original article, I have begun to unpack the anger I was feeling at the time of writing, and to consider why it was so important to me to share my experiences with those who can never really understand them. I live in a city that is supposedly multicultural, but somehow the majority of my networks are white. Partly this is a result of self-selection – as I have discussed elsewhere, beginning at school, I have chosen to build friendships with white people in what I now see as an attempt to separate myself from POC, and to construct myself as more assimilated with the majority culture. The lack of diversity in my friendship groups may also be tied in with having attended schools in the city's wealthiest suburbs, and studying arts at university, which could act as a class filter to a degree. In any case, opportunities to debrief with other POC about experiences of racism have been rare. When they are available, though, they are intensely satisfying.

In 2013, my 'token ethnic friend' (as I jokingly call her) Farz introduced me to a Pakistani-Australian friend of hers, Maryam. All three of us writers, all three of us migrants, we started spending time together regularly. Our conversations ranged from our families to our difficulties in love, to our writing, and back again. We talked about our difference without the anger or the subtle embarrassment that usually casts a shade on similar discussions with white people. We found in each other points of similarity, recognition of our emotions and a validation we could rarely find elsewhere.

At the time, I was working on a few essays exploring some of the darkest times in my relationship with my family, and the culturally constrained life I was leading as a result of my decision to step off the Indian path that had been laid at my feet at birth. I couldn't show these essays to my usual beta readers – three white friends I loved and respected – as they couldn't provide the perspective I needed. I wanted feedback from readers who could analyse the essays through a lens of parental disapproval and social impact – just how damaging might these essays be to my relationship with my family? And did they capture the conflict and confusion of cultural difference I was trying to portray?

Farz and Maryam were able to provide this perspective. We called ourselves the 'Short Brown Literary Ladies', and joked about one day starting a web series depicting the moments when our cultural difference became a burden (like having to get laser hair removal on our thick ethnic moustaches, or having a wardrobe of Good Ethnic Girl clothes that we could wear to family gatherings).

But even as I enjoyed the sense of inclusion and shared experience, I was aware of how the three of us might look to an outsider. Three brown girls together. The similarities we shared were probably not the similarities others assumed in us. I remembered how often customers at our family businesses assumed that my brother was my husband when we worked together as teenagers. And how often my Indian boss at the pharmacy was assumed to be my father. What relationship did people guess existed between Farz, Maryam and me? Were we family friends, cousins, sisters? Were we just three brown people, or an Iranian-Australian, a Pakistani-Australian and a Fijian-Indian-Australian? Were we all 'other', an example of not assimilating? Or was I being paranoid, allowing years of racism to sour the simple enjoyment of time spent with friends?

It was fascinating to discover that I had social needs that hadn't been met for most of my life, and that I hadn't even recognised until now. In particular, it was the sense of solidarity I felt when I was with people who could understand, without requiring elaborate explanation or justification, the experience of being a POC. Crucially, too, these friendships were a space outside of my family, where discussions of racism often felt loaded with our protectiveness of each other, and where discussions of racial identity were rare – perhaps because I am the only member of my family who is preoccupied with this issue.

With white friends, my attempts to discuss race and the ways my life differed from theirs often felt awkward, or as though I was highlighting my difference. At high school I occasionally mentioned music I loved from a recent Bollywood movie, or showed my friends pictures of new Indian outfits I had bought. Once, I showed a close friend a photo of Shah Rukh Khan, the Bollywood actor who I still think is one of the best-looking men alive. Shah Rukh doesn't conform to western standards of attractiveness – his skin is a rich brown, his hair thick and black, his nose bigger than average. But I have always found him dreamy.

When I showed my friend, though, she laughed at me and said he was ugly. She couldn't understand how I could find him attractive. We were swooning over Orlando Bloom and Viggo

Mortensen from *The Lord of the Rings* – men who conformed to western standards of attractiveness at the time. To me, Shah Rukh Khan was just as crush-worthy as those Hollywood heartthrobs. I remember feeling deflated, as though I was somehow incredibly uncool, and that the things that I loved that were Indian were stupid and uninteresting to the people whose opinions I most cared about most deeply.

I can't blame my friends for their dismissal of Indian culture back then – they were teenagers, interested only in the culture they could understand. Besides, I myself felt torn between the things I loved from my culture, and the new things I was coming to love that didn't fit into the framework I had grown up with, such as feminism and indie music. But the experience did spark in me a lifelong furtiveness concerning Indian popular culture, and I began to hide these interests from my non-POC friends, and to distance myself from other Indians in an attempt to show clearly which 'side' I was on. This took me so far to the other side of assimilation, where the boundary between my Indian heritage and my adopted Australian identity became so fixed that I now find it difficult to travel between the two.

In retrospect, I can see that my desire to keep these two identities separate and non-porous was a result of a sort of self-applied prejudice. I had taken my friends' lack of interest in Indian popular culture as a broader statement on Indianness as a whole. Subconsciously deciding that my interest in Bollywood or Indian music was a social liability, I had deliberately disengaged from them. This is a more insidious form of racism. Neither my friends nor I at the time understood the subtler social cues we were following, which lift up white cultures at the same time as they denigrate minority cultures.

The only way minority cultures can come to be seen as 'cool' is via cultural appropriation – that is, by white people who already own 'cultural capital' bestowing their approval on aspects of minority cultures. Think of Gwen Stefani taking the bindi from Hindu culture and wearing it without any reference to its broader symbolism, and in a way that was not accessible to Indian women in the diaspora, who would probably want to continue to attach at least some of the original purpose of the item to its use as a signifier of faith and marital status. Significantly, white people who appropriate symbols of minority cultures do not provide access to POC to own and replicate their cultures for mass consumption themselves, by supporting minority artists or by working to address the barriers that exist for POC artists to operate on the same scale as white artists (barriers of class, of education and of unconscious bias).

This form of appropriation occurs in numerous ways, and has been dissected widely among POC and white people in the media. Personally, I am not against the melting of cultural boundaries, and I think there is value to seeing cultural touch-points from different countries entering into a more global sphere where we can engage with them and hopefully enhance tolerance between cultures. But as it occurs now, the power continues to be in the hands of white people, to take and use aspects of minority cultures while minorities themselves are unable to access the same privilege.

When my friends mocked Shah Rukh Khan, or my Indian clothes, or, later, my inability to dress or party the same way they did, they were inadvertently replicating the systemic erosion of Indian culture that occurred through colonisation, and that extended to the diaspora. Years later, when the same friends dressed up in Indian clothes to attend our university's annual South Asian Students' Society ball (a huge event on the university calendar), I felt frustrated at their sudden approval of glitzy, glamorous saris, when I, who had spent years unpicking the Indian threads of my identity, felt unable to engage with the event without a sense of dissonance.

It's the choice that is afforded to white people that has always troubled me. To choose whether or not to engage with the issue of racism and cultural diversity, to choose whether or not to believe me when I say I have experienced racism, to choose whether or not to see a cultural artefact as cool or not cool – these choices are laden with a power I don't possess.

Recently, my creative white friends have started to feel the discomfort of their privilege more keenly. In the wake of global political events that threaten to erase the progress made to date on issues like racial and gender equality (ahem, Trump, Brexit), my generation is feeling increased pressure to find solutions to cultural inequality.

Let's put to one side the fact that cultural change without systemic change is worthless (I could probably write an entire book about that). The desire of an artist to ensure that their work is representative is usually driven by positive motives. Writer friends have asked me for advice on how to ensure that their depictions of POC characters are inclusive and accurate, and that their representation of Australian society is diverse. For a long time, I have been torn on this issue. On one hand, I want to encourage them and reinforce their desire to be woke in their art. On the other hand, it can irritate me to have to be their cultural spirit guide, especially when I have my own work to focus on.

Further, despite my firm belief in the importance of cultural representation in art and the freedom of artists to explore whatever issues they want to, a part of me feels a secret spark of outrage every time I hear of another white writer covering migrant stories or Indigenous issues in their work. I think, *That is not your story to tell.* This is difficult for me to fe
because I fear censorship of artists, regardless of the mo
tions behind it. I want artists to always be able to expl
issue through their work, regardless of their person
With this in mind, my outrage is somewhat irrat
almost instinctive – it comes from a fear tha

might be taken away from cultures that have already lost so much. I also wonder whether POC artists have the same access to platforms for their work as my white friends have.

What is the duty of both white and POC artists in this regard, to enable cultural change without further solidifying the structures that make it so that white people hold the power in deciding which stories are told? I have supported my creative peers whenever I can by answering questions about my lived experience and engaging in robust discussions on the issues. But recently I've started to feel differently about the best way for white artists to be allies to their POC peers.

One writer spoke to me about wanting to ensure that his characters are representative of the diversity of Australia's population. His work is set in Canberra in a projected future, but the characters are meant to be essentially the same as his existing circle. I found myself wondering about his use of the word 'representation'. He feared that his work would not be representative of reality if all the characters were white. And yet his networks are primarily white. Other than me and some overseas artists he has engaged with through cultural exchanges, this writer is surrounded by whiteness. In a city that has a large multicultural population, this speaks to the inherent exclusiveness of the art world, in which artists are required to have the social mobility, education and English language skills to be able to seek out creative communities, exposure and institutional support for their work. This does not mean that white artists are racist. But it does point to an uncomfortable truth: that while plenty of white artists care deeply about equality for POC, they may not actually *know* any POC.

My advice for this friend was to stop trying to manufacture inclusion through his imaginative works, and to instead write what he knows. If it makes him uncomfortable to confront the whiteness of his friends and peers and his day-to-day life, then it would be worthwhile for him to examine that discomfort, and sit with it. There is value for an artist in self-reflection, and in examining ways to meaningfully address the lack of diversity in his world beyond the fiction he creates.

If he wants to include diverse characters but isn't sure whether it will offend some POC, then he should go forth with that risk in mind, and if it does result in conflict, he should do his best to learn from it. And if he wants to see more diversity in art, he could support the work of POC artists, promote opportunities to as wide a network as possible, and reach out to POC artists whose work he admires to let them know that their work is valuable and meaningful to him. Ultimately, he should engage in this process with openness to his own ignorance of prejudice and discrimination based on race.

It is not the job of POC to both overcome the barriers put in place by a world system that privileges whiteness *and* to support white people as they deal with their own guilt and uncertainty when it comes to cultural diversity. Most POC artists prefer to focus primarily on their own work without having to also perform as an oracle of diversity for well-meaning white artists. This is not to say that I don't appreciate the work white artists are trying to do. I know it must feel tenuous and vulnerable to navigate inequality as the privileged party. It's also crucial to point out that there is a vast array of opinions on this topic among POC in Australia – we are not a homogenous group, and there will always be differences in opinion on a topic this difficult to unpack.

There is no quick fix. There is no short cut. This will take years of education, of policy change, of attitudinal change, of starts and stops and restarts. It will be hard, and sometimes painful for everyone involved. There will be moments of elation, and moments of intense disappointment. There is nothing for it but to try, and to accept failure when it happens, and to keep trying despite it.

~

I had not realised the extent to which many white Australians just don't know what the reality of racism looks like for POC until my feminist journal, *Feminartsy*, hosted a book club on Maxine Beneba Clarke's *The Hate Race* in 2016. Maxine is a source of great inspiration for me, as a POC writer exploring issues around race in Australia, and *The Hate Race* is her memoir of growing up black in Sydney. We had an all-POC panel discussing the book, and the room was packed.

'One thing I loved about this book was the humour,' I commented. My fellow panellists nodded in recognition, but when I looked out at the mainly white audience, I was met with mostly blank stares.

'I found the book really troubling to read,' an audience member said hesitantly. 'I actually was just so shocked by how awful the racism was, I couldn't engage with the humour.'

I paused for a moment, because we had arrived at the same crossroads I had reached with so many of my friends in the past when discussing racism. 'I guess for people of colour like us, those experiences that Maxine explores aren't exactly news,' I said carefully. 'That's just our day-to-day.'

It seemed many readers simply did not understand that Clarke's experience of racism, while certainly unique in its details, is not dissimilar from that of hundreds of migrant families in Australia. This is a reminder to me of how ill-equipped white Australians often are to be supportive allies to POC. If you aren't even aware of the extent of an issue, can you know how to respond to it?

When I revisited the original article I wrote, almost two years later in 2017, I thought that since then I might have uncovered further useful suggestions to offer to white Australians who want to be allies to POC. In a political climate where all minorities need allies more than ever before, I felt I should be able to suggest more concrete, tangible actions that could be taken. But the issue of racism is as elusive as smoke. It is hard to pin down, hard to completely expel – it is layer upon layer of fine ash, so subtle that it is absorbed into our lungs and skin without us even realising.

So the advice I gave in my original article still stands. If your POC friend tells you about a time when someone was racist to them, and you don't know what to say, here's a guide to how to respond:

1. Listen to them.
2. Tell them you're sorry they had to go through that.
3. Ask them if there's anything you can do.
4. Keep listening.

TWICE A STRANGER

I regret not remembering the journey. I have fragments of memories from those early days, but the voyage itself survives nowhere in my mind, not even in my imagination. The most important four hours of my life, the journey that has ultimately defined my every experience and cemented forever the difference between me and my ancestors, is one I have no real connection to.

It is a short flight across the Pacific Ocean from Fiji to Australia. I have since made the trip many times. But that first time, in 1992, was the most significant. With that flight, my family assured forever that our cultural identities would be more complex than before. Now we were not Fijian-Indian, we were Fijian-Indian-Australian, a definition that has never been entirely fixed in place, but instead is constantly in flux.

My earliest memories of Australia itself are of movement. I remember the roll of my pram on cracked footpaths as Mum pushed us both towards the Lavington Shopping Centre. I remember walking with my babysitter, Val, a hearty Australian woman who would point through the flickering sunlight at galahs in the trees, and make me Nutella sandwiches to eat in front of her TV. I remember driving with my father, watching the beaming trail of streetlights slide past the car window. 'I make those,' he told me, and I pictured him in a big workshop, carving wooden posts by hand and creating the magic of light in a dark room.

Australia literally saved my life. I was born with asthma so severe that my parents were told not to expect me to live past three or four years old. When I was born, my mum was quite unwell and needed urgent medical attention, and in the hubbub at the hospital the doctors forgot to mention that my breathing was an issue. A few weeks later, my grandmother, a nurse, was at our house, and on some strange flash of intuition, rushed into the bedroom to check on me, only to find that I had stopped breathing. For the next few years, my asthma was a constant issue, making it difficult for me to eat or sleep, with numerous medical emergencies along the way. I was three when we arrived in Australia, and the healthcare here, so much more robust and available than in Fiji at that time, probably saved me, and allowed me to reach adulthood. Asthma attacks are now a rare occurrence.

Moving to Australia was never spoken of as something that my parents had to deliberate over, in terms of whether or not to leave Fiji. It was seen as a given that when the opportunity arose they would leave, to build lives in one of the developed countries that were our neighbours. The only real question was whether to move to Australia, as yet unknown to us, or New Zealand, where both my parents had attended university. I have never questioned the logic of this inevitability. Conversations with my parents about migration only ever referenced the obvious benefits of leaving Fiji, and the evident desire of extended family still living in Fiji also to leave.

Recently, idling in a cafe with my mother, I asked her where she would live if she could choose anywhere in the world.

Without any hesitation, she said, 'Fiji.'

'I meant somewhere good, Mum, like anywhere at all,' I said without thinking.

She smiled patiently at me, in a way I now recognise is born from her wisdom, as compared to my youthful arrogance, and said, 'Fiji is my home. If I could live like I do in Australia in Fiji, I would.'

It was the first time I had considered the possibility that, given the chance to live free from the tumultuousness of ongoing political conflict, and with access to a flourishing economy and high living standards, my parents would have wanted to stay in the community they grew up in. Migration is so normalised in Fijian-Indian culture that it's easy to lose sight of how massive a transition it is, from one country to another.

Moving to Australia vastly improved our lives in some ways, but it also came at a cost. My parents left their families, their friends, their language, the traditions and customs that made sense to them, and came to a place where they endured racism and hostility, all while being expected to be grateful and never criticise their adopted home.

When, as a teenager, I referred to myself as 'Australian', my parents would sometimes add 'Fijian-Indian'. This insistence on holding onto our Fijian identity always seemed irrelevant to me. Sometimes, I saw it as my parents trying to reinforce the very differences that I was yearning to hide. I wanted to be as Australian as possible, not realising that that very desire was what my parents feared for their children – a loss of heritage.

During a conversation with my father, I asked him what he would have done if he hadn't become an engineer. A man of many interests, my father has two degrees, and has started another, all in diverse fields. I assumed that he had had numerous ambitions as a young man, and engineering just won out.

'I would be a teacher,' he told me.

I was surprised. I had never heard him express any interest in teaching – in fact, when he helped us with our homework, it almost always ended in frustration and tears, when he pushed too hard or we became bored and mutinous.

'I had no idea you wanted to be a teacher,' I said. 'Why didn't you study teaching?'

'No, I mean I would have had to be a teacher. It's the only other career you could easily have in Fiji, unless you study overseas, that's more white-collar.'

My father came from a poor family with nine children. A career in the few other white-collar professions available in Fiji, such as the civil service, would have been out of his reach. But his grades won him a scholarship to study engineering, so that's what he did. His personal goals and ambitions had little to do with it.

Nothing could illustrate the difference between my parents' experiences as migrants and my own more clearly than my recent move to Scotland. In June 2017, Chris and I took the path trodden by many young Australians before us, heading off to spend some time in the bonnie UK. In our case, this has led to us settling in Edinburgh for just under a year. As I write this, I am four months in. During this time, I have become uncomfortably aware of the stark contrast between this journey and the one my parents took 25 years ago to Australia.

Where my parents were driven to emigrate to seek better economic opportunities and a stronger education for their children, my move is a direct result of their achieving these goals. My tertiary qualifications and affluence mean that I can choose to leave a well-paid senior management role and transport myself, my belongings and even my cat to another country on little more than a whim, and with no long-term plan to stay here. This individualism and mobility are products of my life in Australia – an existence grounded in consistency and egalitarianism, and the notion of a 'fair go' for all. Unlike my parents, I have not had to consider a politically unstable environment, the difficulty of finding permanent work, the need to provide for my family back home, or how to negotiate cultural differences. I am fluent in English, but more importantly, I speak it with a western accent. I wear white people's clothes, and I even have a real live white person with me most of the time, further emphasising the rightness of my being here.

Did my parents know that when they brought me as a toddler from Fiji to Australia they were gently stimulating the tentative growth of new wings, which would eventually carry me far away from them? Can they understand my own move, motivated entirely by fancy and a desire to experience something different, as anything other than frivolous? In moving from one white country to another, I have shed my skin as a 'migrant' and instead taken on the label of privilege and superiority as an 'expatriate'.

They weren't lying about the rain in Edinburgh. This place is so wet, there is even a special word, 'dreich', for the kind of drizzle that is too light to fall to the ground and instead hangs in the air, drenching you and everything around you.

I have just bought a car for £200, a transaction that makes me question the safety of driving it. We've been living in our new flat in the suburb of Northfield for a few weeks. It is a quiet block, classified as a 'new build' (which means built in the last century or so). I am yet to meet any of our neighbours, but apparently today is the day.

I am rushing towards my car in the residents' carpark, the hood of my jacket pulled up against the rain. Just as I reach my car, a loud voice booms at me from somewhere in the vicinity of the sky, 'You cannae park there!'

I look around in confusion before realising that the voice belongs to a red-faced, middle-aged Scottish man, leaning out of his window, which is directly below my own flat.

'Excuse me?' I yell over the rain.

'You cannae park there unless you live here. Move your car!'

'I do live here!'

'No you don't, that's my car spot!'

I check. It definitely has my apartment number painted in front of it.

'That's my apartment,' I call back. 'I live in number eight!'

'No, you don't!'

This is just silly, I decide. Who is this old white guy to tell me where I live? 'I do live here! Do you want to see my lease agreement?' I shout, determined not to back down, especially if he's insinuating something racist.

'Well . . . don't hit my car when you open that door!'

'I know how to open a fucking car door!' I yell back, and tear the door open to demonstrate.

I screech out of the carpark, my hand extended out the window so I can flip him off, just as Chris pops his head out of our window to see what's going on. I am shaking, and so angry my rage is fogging up the windows of the car. How dare that man tell me I can't park my car in the spot allocated to my apartment? How dare he insist I don't live there, as if perhaps I've forgotten my own address and am wandering around aimlessly in car parks like a well-dressed tramp?

Underneath my anger, though, is a small spark of vindication. I've been waiting for this. Since I arrived in Edinburgh, I've been keeping my ears pricked and my eyes peeled, hackles always raised, waiting for the first experience of racism. It must come eventually, I tell myself. This place can't be that different from Australia, where I encounter casual racism at least fortnightly, if not weekly. Scotland is, after all, one of the few countries I have been to where white people really were there first (at least in recorded history and to the best of our knowledge). Some Scottish people must feel even more entitled and even less tolerant of immigration than those Australians who wilfully ignore the fact that the land they cling to so staunchly was stolen in the first place. And yet the only reactions I have experienced from Scots are either ambivalence or extreme friendliness. In fact, my accent is sometimes mistaken as English, and I often get asked for directions. Clearly Indians have been here long enough for our appearance to be incorporated into the characteristics expected from a Brit. We are one of the 'model migrant' groups, an insidious term that always makes me think about how things rarely stay in fashion for long. This strange man's outburst has rectified an imbalance, put me back on familiar territory. Anger I can handle. The silence of the Scots is what spooks me.

When my parents emigrated, they did so with a totality of risk – either this worked or our family would be in significant trouble. There wasn't a fallback plan. My father had to make his job work, no matter how bad the conditions were or how much he hated it. Mum had to find a new job as well, from the limited options available in Albury. Regardless of the community we found, or the difficulty of saving for a home, getting us kids settled in school and still finding time to enjoy our lives here, the single goal was always to make it work.

My parent's finances have always been limited to what they can genuinely create themselves. Their hard work has paved the way for their children, and is directly related to my own move now. In the lead-up to moving to Scotland, I remarked flippantly to friends that there really wasn't a downside to our journey. 'What's the worst that can happen?' I said, waving a hand casually in the air. 'If we really fuck it up, our parents will bail us out.' This is true. It's not a scenario that I ever want to actually have to deal with, but the fact is that if I hadn't found work, or had miscalculated the set-up costs, or for any other reason we couldn't make ends meet, my parents would help me. If for some reason they couldn't, I have siblings who could help me financially. Or, if I needed to take a small loan from an Australian bank to tide me over, my decent salary means I could easily pay off my debt. It is a remarkably freeing situation to be in.

I wonder sometimes if my parents ever reflect on how their hard work has almost enabled me not to have to work hard at all. The type of work that I do is a choice, and I can focus my energy on pursuing personal goals instead of the business of making ends meet. Had they known, is this the outcome they would have chosen – that their child could frivolously make life decisions to chase experiences, not opportunities?

I wonder if the choices I make ever seem ridiculous to them. At my age they had four children and a house in Fiji, and were saving every penny to move to another country. I spend stupid amounts of money on entertainment and eating out, and even paid thousands of dollars to take my cat overseas with me. This is such a stark sign of privilege, it's hard for me to talk about it with my parents without feeling a small kernel of discomfort at the extent to which my freedom is a result of their sacrifice.

I wonder, if I was in their position, whether I could live my life guided not by my own desires but by a desire to create more opportunity and freedom for my offspring. In fact, the thought of having children terrifies me, precisely because I can't imagine being as selfless as my parents have been.

Part of me also wonders what message my flight from Australia implicitly conveys. My family's emigration from Fiji was momentous and consequential, undoubtedly the root cause of our success, education and economic stability now. To leave this country that my parents brought us to, and where they patiently and stoically carved out a life for us, for another western, first-world country seems an arbitrary dismissal of their gift.

My goals – to see more of the world, to experience a mildly different culture and set my life against a slightly different environmental backdrop – seem immature compared to my parents' goal: removing their children from Fiji's political and economic instability and placing us in a culture that opened up literally a world of opportunities.

My decisions are selfish in more ways than one – they are based primarily on my desire to experience different things, but also, crucially, they have implications only for myself. When I earn money, it is for myself. How I live in Scotland is defined by my own means, my own willingness to work a certain number of hours, and my own preferred living standards. I am not answerable to anyone else for how I live my life. (Even though Chris and I live together, our finances are separate enough that if we were to part ways, we would each simply continue to be responsible for our own lives.) But my parents' financial decisions had implications for their family in

Australia, Fiji and elsewhere. As is expected in our culture of those who have successfully emigrated, they have always sent money back to our relatives in Fiji and India.

Their move was meaningful and permanent – they were truly building a life in another country. The most striking difference between our respective journeys is that I have left with every intention of returning to the country that feels most like home to me. But my parents left knowing that, should citizenship of Australia be granted, they would willingly renounce their Fijian citizenship and stay in Australia for the remainder of their lives. There was no discussion around this, no weighing up of pros and cons – it was the entire point of the move. Even if they found Australia to be a terrible place to live, where they made no networks and found no community, we would have stayed. My parents made a true journey, while I am merely taking a break, a short trip away from my reality, safe in the knowledge that there is an easy pathway back whenever I am ready.

Since coming to Scotland, I have become embarrassingly patriotic. To the complete surprise of Chris and my Australian friend Courtney, I regularly begin sentences with 'In Australia . . .' to introduce a denigration of whatever British thing is currently irking me, and a detailed explanation of how Australia deals with the same issue much more effectively. I pounce on anyone with a hint of an Antipodean accent to ask whether they're from Australia or New Zealand (though I pride myself on generally being able to tell the difference). Even while surrounded by the beauty, history and novelty of Edinburgh, I find myself wistfully thinking of the Brindabella mountains, the scent of eucalyptus and the comforting sight of a mob of kangaroos through the hazy springtime morning light. In this new culture that so often spins my head with its minor yet unavoidable differences from home, I claim my Australian heritage without any hesitation (although often with a disclaimer noting that I disagree with offshore detention centres and the treatment of Indigenous Australians).

Patriotism is not a feeling I have experienced before. If anything, the word has sinister connotations for me, conjuring up images of young men draped in the Australian flag marching the streets in search of POC to beat up. I think of the 2005 Cronulla riots, the 'love it or leave it' stickers on the backs of cars, and Pauline Hanson's rhetoric about Australia as a place for white people where anyone not seen as suitable can be deported on command.

The thought of being patriotic in Australia is alien to me. I am both automatically apologetic about and, by extension, frustrated by the way our current government addresses issues of inequality across the board, including race, culture, sexuality, gender and ability. The knowledge that, as a migrant, I benefit from the colonisation of the country, including the genocide of its First Peoples, and that in many ways I contribute to the ongoing oppression of those people through my participation in the capitalist democracy that governs our country, makes it hard for me to claim my Australianness without also confronting the invalidity of it. Yet, in Edinburgh, safe from the sceptical looks of other Australians, my patriotic pride has flourished into nothing short of an obsession. I tell people that Australia has the best beaches/wildlife/coffee/brunch in the world. I use 'fang' as a verb ('fang a left there', 'fang me a muffin, please'), and actually said g'day without irony the other day.

Perhaps what I enjoy most about my renewed love of my country is that Scots accept my Australian identity without question – and when I tell them I'm Australian, not a single person has asked me where I'm 'really from'. I can't be proud of my Australian identity in Australia, because a day rarely passes without another Australian questioning it. In Australia, to claim my citizenship is always a challenge, never a given. When I say I'm Australian, I'm aware that I am pushing against centuries of history in which that term was withheld from immigrants and Indigenous Australians, and applied to white people in staggered tiers. There is a scale of Australianness, and your place on it is defined by arbitrary factors, including your wealth, your arrival date and your skin colour.

The UK has its own race problems, but Indians are no longer a primary target. Instead, when I notice subtle racism, it's directed at Eastern Europeans, and I feel a pang of guilt, mingled with relief at being out of the firing line. There has never been a flicker of doubt from anyone I've met in the UK, whether they are white themselves or not, that I am Australian and that I have a right to claim that identity. If further details of my ethnic heritage are discussed, it's usually a result of a genuine conversation that has somehow touched on cultural experiences.

It is sad and yet not unbelievable that I feel more Australian when half a world away from Australia. It tells me a lot about how non-Australians see our cultural identity, and how different it is from the tales we tell ourselves. I question whether my fierce pride in my country will last when I return home. I wonder how long it will take before I am asked again to justify my presence in Australia, and before I have to add the hyphens back to my identity, as an Indian-Fijian-Australian.

I wonder if I will be able to remember the yearning I feel for home right now, or if the mountains, the oceans and the towering grey gum trees will feel flat and unenticing when I am once again immersed in the race politics that so often force me to step back from feeling Australian. Perhaps being Australian is a state of mind for me – accessible through the portal of distance, but one that wobbles and blurs when I am too close to home.

I am waiting on the kerb outside our apartment block for an Uber, my phone in my hand, my foot tapping with impatience. A red car rolls out of the carpark next to me, and a horn blares. I jump and turn to see Alan waving jovially from the driver's window. I grin/grimace back and wave a hand reluctantly. He careens out of the driveway and down the road, every curve of his lovingly polished car gleaming.

Alan is the man who yelled at me out of the window, accusing me of not living here. After this rough start, though, he has been eager to secure our friendship. The day after the slanging match, Chris and I answered a knock on our door to see him standing there with a grin and a box of chocolates. For over fifteen minutes, he apologised in an accent so thick we could barely understand him. Eventually his apologies turned into a long history of his career, the fact that he has a room full of guns that he likes to take out for game shooting, his opinion of Australia, and so on.

Eventually, we managed to wave him off, but since then he stops to chat whenever we run into him in the hallway, and I occasionally hear a knock on our door that I stoically ignore, sure it's Alan offering to lend us a DVD, or wanting to tell us about the restaurant he went to last night. Putting aside the exhausting nature of his conversation (it's less a conversation and more a verbal onslaught, to be honest), I also just feel awkward about interacting with Alan.

I still feel sheepish about my strong reaction to our first encounter. Over the past few weeks I have had to concede that he probably wasn't actually being racist. It's clear to me now that Alan is strange, and possibly a little unhinged (his detailed descriptions of his guns and their individual shooting ranges make me more than a little nervous), but not particularly prejudiced. Now that I've seen how much he genuinely adores his car, I realise that his only thought was to protect it from being scratched.

So why was I so quick to assume he was being racist? In part, I wanted my unspoken fear of rejection by this country to be proven well-founded. I don't want to believe that only Australia is plagued with casual racism – or, worse, that the casual racism in Scotland is directed at another victim and I am the unwitting beneficiary of this targeted prejudice. It was also somewhat related to my desire to start my journey in the UK off on the right foot, by standing up to any racism or discrimination I experience here instead of scuttling away, my usual response in Australia.

All it took was to hear Alan's raised voice from the window for adrenalin to flood my veins, and for me to yell back at him with equal vigour. Now, realising that I probably misunderstood much of what he said (given that I can hardly understand him when he's a few inches away from me), I am ashamed of my own response, and the middle finger I held up as I drove away.

Today, I try to push these thoughts out of my mind as I climb into the Uber and greet the driver. We start chatting about Uber, and the gig economy. The driver has a very Edinburgh accent – a little milder than Glaswegian and about a billion times easier for me to understand than the Borders or Highland accents. He is brown-skinned like me, and I am guessing his ethnic origin is South Asian.

'I used to work for a power company,' he tells me, as he explains how he became a taxi driver. 'But they were racist.

They never promoted any of us that wasn't white. We even tried to put a complaint in – we picked a mixed-race guy to be our spokesperson. But they just promoted him, and nothing else ever happened.' His tone is bitter, and I remember hearing the same tone in my father's voice when I occasionally asked about some of the racism he experienced working as an engineer.

'You know, it's damned if you do, damned if you don't,' the driver goes on. 'We grow up here, our kids grow up here, but we never stop being discriminated against. And then the kids don't even speak our language, know our culture.'

'It's tough,' I commiserate. 'I didn't realise how important Indian culture would be to me until I got older, but my parents tried really hard when I was a kid.'

'Yeah, it's hard to do both,' he says.

We start to talk about conflict and racism. He mentions that he is Punjabi, and I explain that I am Gujarati – two states often assumed to be fierce rivals in India.

'You know, most violence in the world is just down to religion,' he says, shrugging. 'I mean, the Muslims might burn down a *mandir* [temple], but the Hindus will get on a train and stab every woman wearing a hijab, you know?' This is literally true, events having occurred exactly like this and in this order in India. The religious riots that have occurred in India throughout history are brutal, and are most often instigated by political party goons to create content for an ideological campaign by one of the Hindu or Muslim candidates.

When we pull up at my destination, we're talking about how each generation of Indians in our adopted countries will be more assimilated than the last, and so on, until there is no such thing as 'race' when it comes to multicultural communities. We will all just be. Neither of us is certain if this will be a good thing. Eventually, I have to pull myself away.

'Good chats,' I tell him as I step out, and he gives me a thumbs-up.

Strange, that in four months of living in Edinburgh, one of the most meaningful conversations I have had is with a stranger in a car, the only common factor the colour of our skin. I pull my coat closer around myself, and turn to walk up the street to where I am meeting a friend for coffee.

In many ways I feel less foreign here than I do at home. Edinburgh is a city of flux, in a country where the borders are porous and the population is only a quarter the size of Australia's. There are so many people from different nationalities moving in and out of the city all the time that the notion of 'cultural identity' feels more flexible, or perhaps less important.

I wonder what my grandparents would have thought when they were young, if they could have known that their descendants would end up scattered across the UK, Australia, New Zealand, India and Fiji. That we would have relatives in Canada and Kenya, and that their grandchildren would speak English with more confidence than Hindi. I wonder if they would have encouraged their children onto planes, or if they would have held them back, made their worlds insular and small so they could retain the essence of who they are.

I wonder who I will be when I return home. Whether I will have added a nugget of Scottish attitudes and philosophies to my Australian, Indian and Fijian core. I wonder if there will one day be a word for a no-nation, no-country person.

ACKNOWLEDGEMENTS

This book is the culmination of years of mulling over these issues, having rants about cultural identities in various cafes and sending rough drafts to friends to help me figure out some of the complex issues I discuss here.

Thank you to my most trusted first readers and friends, Melissa Wellham and Ashley Thomson, for your feedback and support, and for gently telling me when I needed to work a little harder with my words. Thank you to my friends and champions, Madalein Tier, Alexis Rosenberg, Isabelle Gath, Katherine Quinn, Julia Braguina, Lauren Montanez, Farz Edraki and Courtney Lawler.

My agent, Grace Heifetz from Curtis Brown Australia, has been an incredible supporter and advisor – may we send cute dog photos via email for many years to come. To my publisher, Robert Watkins, and editor, Sophie Mayfield, at Hachette Australia, and to copyeditor Clara Finlay – I have felt very safe in your experienced hands.

To my partner, Chris, you know what you mean to me, and your patience and support is everything. Our cat, Bella, has been a crucial writing companion, so thank you to RSPCA ACT for bringing her into our lives.

And finally, my family have made me who I am, supported my writing from as soon as I could grip a pencil, and have been tremendously generous in allowing me to share some of our lives in these pages. Mum, Abba, Zaved, Zaheeda and Zakia, I love you so much and I can't thank you enough. And to my nieces and nephew, Umaiza, Zain, Zara, Arya and Amira, all my love forever.

NOTES

THE LABOUR OF A MIGRANT

1. V Chok, 'Yellow', in N Skukla (ed), *The Good Immigrant*, Unbound, United Kingdom, 2017, p. 43.

LIVING A HYPHENATED LIFE

2. D Chew-Bose, *Too Much and Not the Mood: Essays*, Farrar, Straus and Giroux, New York, 2017, p. 161.
3. C Ngozi Adichie, *Americanah*, HarperCollins, New York, 2013, p. 209.

MONEY CAN'T BUY HARMONY

4. S Burns, 'In Defence of the Bad, White Working Class', *Meanjin*, Winter 2017.
5. Ibid.
6. K Malik, 'Away with the Gatekeepers', Pandaemonium, 16 October 2014, viewed 26 February 2018, https://kenanmalik.wordpress.com/2016/04/14/away-with-the-gatekeepers/.

7. *Q&A*, television program, ABC, Sydney, 13 February 2017.
8. Malik, Pandaemonium.

WHEN 'CHAI' IS 'TEA', AND 'CHAI TEA' IS 'TEA TEA'

9. N Shukla, 'Namaste', *The Good Immigrant*, Unbound, United Kingdom, 2017, p. 1.
10. Ibid.

AGAINST THE TIDE

11. J Aglionby, 'Four Times as Many Women Died in Tsunami', *The Guardian*, 26 March 2005, viewed 4 April 2018, https://www.theguardian.com/society/2005/mar/26/internationalaidanddevelopment.indianoceantsunamidecember2004.

BIDDING THE *BIDAAI* – MARRIAGE, FAREWELLS AND FEMINISM

12. B Sinha, 'The Adverse Effects of the Western Fixation on India's "Rape Problem"', *Berkeley Political Review*, 10 November 2015, viewed 23 March 2017, https://bpr.berkeley.edu/2015/11/10/focusing-on-indias-rape-problem-is-a-problem.

HOW TO BE AN ALLY TO PEOPLE OF COLOUR – TAKE TWO

13. R Eddo-Lodge, 'Why I'm No Longer Talking to White People About Race', 22 February 2014, viewed 23 March 2017, http://renieddolodge.co.uk/why-im-no-longer-talking-to-white-people-about-race.
14. Ibid.